The Gun Free Killing Zones Of America

By

Stephen C. Challis

Contents

This book is dedicated to my wife and soul mate Eva, whose dedication and long hours spent editing and fact checking have made it all possible.

The Killing Zones of America

By Stephen Challis

The anti -gun crowd is leading the victims to these killers, like sheep to a slaughter you read me right. I now, after the last 20 years of multiple murder-suicide, how could anyone in their right mind believe otherwise? By labeling certain "gun free zones" what they have actually done is unwittingly create something that wackos translate into "target rich environment " or "defenseless sheep ; killed here."

'From Luby's to the Legislature' by Suzzana Gratia Hupp

Introduction

Most people in Europe look to the United States as a unique example of a country where freedom and the right of self- determination are foremost in the nation's legal system. The anchor to those freedoms is the Bill of Rights.

These 10 commandments not only form part of The United States Constitution, which guarantees the freedom of it citizens, they are the very foundation on which the country was established.

The Second Amendment gives those same citizens the Right to own and use arms to defend themselves and their families. In this, The United States of America is almost unique. Most western countries have various controls in force to limit the possession and use of firearms by private citizens.

In fact The United Kingdom, America's closest ally has banned the ownership of handguns by private citizens in all but a few instances, (for more on the UK situation see *"Debarred the use of Arms" Outskirts Publishing 2012*)

With the Second Amendment in force and very much guarded, despite the activities of various anti- gun (anti- constitutional) groups, one could be forgiven for thinking that the US citizen would feel very secure in his belief that he could defend himself anywhere within our borders. That assumption would be wrong.

There are a large number of areas in the country where the right to self- defense does not exist where carrying a firearm is likely to lead to arrest and imprisonment.

More importantly these areas are the cause of very high murder rates. In short, these areas are killing Zones, where our most vulnerable citizens, our children, are put at risk by the policies of misguided lawmakers who put money and politics before safety.

These areas are The Government established Gun Free Zones where armed criminals can freely operate, safe in the knowledge that their victims are unable to fight back equally.

The Gun Free School Zones Act 1990 was enacted under section 1702 of the Gun Control Act 1990. It was, like most of the anti-gun legislation, promoted as a sensible precautionary law to keep children and other vulnerable people safe from guns.

Schools were made gun free zones and teachers, pupils, public and criminals were told that they could not carry guns within 1000 feet of those premises. (Anyone see a flaw in this program?)

Ok! So far - so good. Teachers, the public, and most pupils complied. Criminals as usual ignored the law (That is why they are called criminals. Duh!), but took note that they would be safe from any armed defense when committing a crime in these areas. The NRA was however not so happy and seeing the dangers immediately campaigned against them. But to no avail the zones stayed in place. The carnage that followed was both horrific and predictable.

In this book I have pulled no punches. The deaths of numerous innocent children and others are blamed firmly and squarely on the legislators who passed these laws. Will these people ever be brought to account? I doubt it.

Can we do something about it?
Well! We can ensure they are voted out of office and are never again placed in the position of putting our citizens and children at risk again.

But this book is not just meant to sound an alarm on gun free zones, nor is it intended to be another book promoting gun rights. This book, I hope will sound alarm bells all over the USA.

It will, I hope, awaken the country to the clear and present danger it faces from overseas. The USA has the strongest armed forces in the world. But they were powerless to prevent 911.

My good friend Lt. Col. Dave Grossman told this story at a seminar that I attended in Ohio in 2011.

About a month after the 9-11 terrorist attacks he was training a group of special operations troops who were headed to Afghanistan.

A Special Forces (Green Beret) sergeant came up during one of the breaks and said, "Colonel, we're going to Afghanistan, and we're gonna kick their tails. While we're over there, you tell all those folks you teach, don't let them come kill our kids."

Well this soldier knew too well the risks to our country. The truth is, this country is facing a real and direct threat. The mastermind of the attack on Pearl Harbor, Japanese Admiral Isoroku Yamamoto is reported to have stated, 'You cannot invade America, because there would be a rifle behind every blade of grass.' While there is scant evidence that this often-quoted truism was actually uttered by the celebrated Admiral, the accuracy of the statement is difficult to deny.

An invading foreign army would face not only the formidable might of the US armed forces, but also an armed population that would resist an enemy soldier attempting to disarm them more violently than the local armed authorities in defense of themselves and family. It is fairly clear therefore that disarming of the American people is essential for anyone wishing to harm us.

This concept was well understood by Adolf Hitler, Josef Stalin, and a large percentage of historical despots. What should also be understood is that there may well be a political reason for the push by various gun control groups, which has nothing to do with safety.

In short, be careful for what you wish for, it may come true. So! With that in mind, let us begin with an assessment of these risks, analyze the evidence of the risks we face and why we should all be concerned.

Chapter 1

The Gathering Storm

When I say that terrorism is war against civilization, I may be met by the objection that terrorists are often idealists pursuing worthy ultimate aims -- national or regional independence, and so forth. I do not accept this argument. I cannot agree that a terrorist can ever be an idealist, or that the objects sought can ever justify terrorism. The impact of terrorism, not merely on individual nations, but on humanity as a whole, is intrinsically evil, necessarily evil and wholly evil.

BENJAMIN NETANYAHU

We must go back to the 70s to see the first stirrings of a serious threat to the children of the United States. The Middle East has been a hotbed of insurrection for many years.

The formation of an independent state of Israel in 1948 caused massive resentment in the region with the fledgling state being immediately attacked by its neighbors, determined to achieve by force what they had been unable to at the negotiating table.

11

What became known as the Arab-Israeli war started off well for the Arab coalition, led by Egypt, with support from Jordon and Syria. The Israeli forces were approximately 29.000 men and a mix match of weapons. Arrayed against them was a combined Arab force of 23,000 men from Egypt, Jordon, Iraq, and Syria, plus a few thousand volunteers.

Great Britain tried to act as peacekeepers, under the umbrella of the United Nations. This led to some bad mistakes, in a war of attrition where the lines between friend and foe were blurred at best. In one celebrated incident, an Israeli air force squadron that was sent to intercept Egyptian units shooting up a train were beaten to the scene by a squadron of British RAF Spitfires, who arrived too late to stop the attack. Unfortunately, at the time, Egypt was also using Spitfires, while Israel was equipped with the ME109 fighter of Germany from WW2. Some were flown by veteran Ex-Battle of Britain, Jewish pilots. The Israeli planes fell on the rookie RAF pilots blasting most of them out of the sky, until frantic radio calls got through and stopped the attack.

The mistake was understandable, both sides used the British Spitfire aircraft sold to them after WW2, and Israel even used the Czech built ME 109.

The Israeli air force also had many wartime pilots from allied countries, including from the USA 182, from South Africa 80, from Canada 53 and from the UK 50. Many were former pilots in the RAF. On that day they found themselves in a dogfight with similar planes being used by each side and being flown by friend and enemy alike.

This sort of confusion dominated most of the fledgling years of the State of Israel. The war dragged on for a year. By the time an armistice had been signed in 1949 Israel had lost 6,373 men. The Arabs lost between 8,000 and 15,000 men.

More importantly the seeds had been sown for a simmering long-term resentment in the region, a resentment which continues to this day. During those hectic and convoluted days, many animosities and friendships were formed. A clash of Islamic and Christian values aroused old enmities dating back to the crusades.

Though the war was over, the guns did not fall silent. By the end of 1948 the Israeli forces had risen to 108,300. Unable to challenge them on the battlefield, embittered Palestinians turned to guerrilla tactics aimed mainly at the civilian population.

The first attack deliberately targeting children was an attack by the "Popular Front for the Liberation Organization General Command" (PLOGC) on an Israeli school bus on May 8, 1970. It marked a new and frightening campaign by Islamic extremists and one which was destined to be repeated again and again in the following years.

The attack in which 12 Israeli civilians were killed, nine of them children, and 25 were wounded, took place on the road to Moshav Avivim, near Israel's border with Lebanon. The deadly ambush was prepared on the children in the name of Allah. As the bus reached the ambush point two anti -tank shells were fired at it from a bazooka.
The terrorists then opened fire with AK-47 automatic weapons from both sides of the road. The driver was amongst those hit in the initial hail of gunfire as were the two other adults on board. All three were killed and the bus crashed into an embankment. The attackers continued shooting into the vehicle, killing 7 children aged 10 and under.
Having achieved their mission, the murderous trio then fled back over the border into the safety of Lebanon, The attack was deadly and merciless, and it also brought the name of the "Popular Front for the Liberation of Palestine General Command" to the front pages of every newspaper in the free world. The attackers were never apprehended.

But a new chapter in inhumanity had been written. From that day, children and unarmed civilians were seen as not only legitimate targets, but preferred targets.

The children who died were buried in a special plot in the Town of Safed, which would again feature in another attack 4 years later.

A monument commemorating the victims of the attack stands in the middle of the Moshav. It names the children and shows their ages.

	Ester Avikezer, 23	Shimon Biton, 9
A	Yehuda Ohayon, 10	Shulamit Biton, 9
	Yafa Batito, 8	Machluf Biton, 28
	Mimon Biton, 7	Aliza Peretz, 14
	Haviva Biton, 7	Rami Yarkoni, 29
	Chana Biton, 8	Shimon Azran, 35

silent testimony that would be repeated again and again, questions of why and disbelief, echoes of which still reverberated 42 years later on the other side of the world at an small Elementary school in Newtown Connecticut called Sandy Hook.

The "Popular Front for the liberation of Palestine General Command" was founded in 1968 as a splinter group of the "Popular Front for the Liberation of Palestine." Both groups were part of the "Palestine Liberation Organization" (PLO).

Although its stated political aim was to create an independent State of Palestine in the Middle East, its actual aim was the destruction of the State of Israel. To this end it had no scruples against targeting the most helpless and vulnerable members of humankind.

All three groups used terrorism and murder to further their agenda. Mostly the targets were so called; "soft targets" such as schools, shopping centers, and restaurants were they could be sure of a high body count with low risk of retaliation. But the most nefarious of all these groups was the Al-Aqsa Martyrs Brigade. It became synonymous with mindless terror attacks on the Jewish State. In the Jewish enclave of Avraham Avinu in Hebron, a Palestinian terrorist named Mahmoud Mahmed Mahmoud Amrou set up a sniper position with an AK-47 assault rifle and took careful aim at a mother and father walking with a stroller. In the stroller was their baby daughter. She was 10 months old.

Mahmoud had three targets in front of him. The parents were the easiest targets. But Instead Mahmoud took aim and shot 10-month-old Shalhevet Pas through the head. Because of the angle, the shot passed through the stroller and struck Pas's father in the legs. By any account this attack had no military or political value. The adults were young.

Her father capable of military service and her mother could still have more children. Even from the twisted tactical standpoint of a terrorist, they were far better targets. But Shalhevet Pass, the 10-month-old baby girl was the one he shot in the head.

Mahmoud Amrou was no random serial killer. He was a member of the Tanzim militia, a terrorist arm of the Palestinian Authority which crosses over extensively with the Al-Aqsa Martyrs Brigade. He confessed that the attack had been ordered by Tanzim and Al-Aqsa commander Marwan Zaloum. The terrorist atrocities of these Fatah terrorist groups were backed at the highest level of the Palestinian Authority.

The murder of the 10 month old had not just been a random killing. It was another act of terror from the Palestinian Authority's own terrorist organization. Many of whose members had actually been armed and trained by Western security forces anxious to target leaders and regimes seen hostile to the west. It is also an inconvenient fact that among the radicals armed in this way by America was a young muslin leader named **Osama Bin Laden**.

It was part of an Islamic terrorist strategy targeting Israeli families and their children, which goes back for over 50 years of atrocities.

In March 2002, in Jerusalem, at a Bar Mitzvah, a celebration was winding down. It was a quiet Sabbath evening. Outside the venue, mothers stood waiting with their children in strollers. The strange man mingled with them, his top coat wrapped tightly around his upper body. Beneath his coat was hidden a suicide bomb vest. The bomber worked his way through the crowd to get himself as close as he could to the children. Then he detonated the vest. The blast killed a family of 6 plus another mother and her 7-year-old son. The mothers and their children had been deliberately targeted. Most of the murdered were Mizrahi Jews who had fled Muslim countries and returned to their Jewish homeland, only to die with their children in front of a synagogue the innocent victims of Muslim terrorists. The wanton attacks continued unabated.

The following year two Muslim terrorists were arrested while planning to detonate a 20-pound explosive belt outside the entrance of a junior high school. The blast was timed for the end of the school day when all the children were leaving. The targeting of children was not only for revenge, the terrorists knew that such killings would cause the maximum anguish among the Israeli nation. In Israel, all citizens are considered soldiers, and military service is compulsory.
This is why holding Israelis hostages have never proved profitable to terrorists.

Take the raid on Entebbe in Uganda, when Israeli commandos stormed the airport and killed all the terrorists. Ugandan soldiers sent to help the terrorists were stopped and all but wiped out buy the elite Israeli rear guard, all but one of the hostages were released, the remaining one was not at the airport and in a hospital, where Ugandan Dictator Idi Amin ordered her murder following the raid.

One Israeli commander died. By all military accounts this was a spectacular rescue. It also sent a message to the terrorists around the world. They changed tactics and instead of targeting military targets they started to attack the children and innocents.

On April 11th, 1974 three terrorists crossed the border from Lebanon. The date match was not a coincidence. The 11th day of the month is a popular date for Muslim terrorist attacks. The World Trade Center was hit on September 11th and Madrid on March 11th. The reason is not too well understood in the west, but roughly can be equated thus:

In Arabic the numerical value of Mohammed adds up to 92. In the Koran, Surah 47 is known as the Surah of Mohammed and it has 38 verses. Add 9 + 2 and you get 11. Add 4 to 7 and you get 11.

Add 3 to 8 and you also get 11. Take the 99 names of Allah and divide them by 9, another key number in Islam, and you get 11. (The numerical value of Allah is 66). These seem like trivial things-- yet thousands of people have died because of the number of letters in Mohammed's name and the number of verses in his Surah in the Koran. A reminder of how indivisible even the trivial numbers in the Koran are from the slaughter carried out on its instructions.

The target of the 3 terrorists was the settlement of Kiryat Shmona, their target that day was an elementary school named Janusz Korczak, but the Muslim lack of knowledge of the Israeli religion was to prove a problem for the fanatical killers. April 11th was Passover and the school building was empty. Therefore its pupils were all away enjoying the holiday vacation. Frustrated, the terrorists invaded a nearby apartment building, where the occupants were armed, and when the fighting was over, 8 children and as many adults lay dead.

A month later, the next effort at a school massacre was more successful. After cutting a hole in the border fence, another terrorist gang entered the town of Ma'alot and pounded on apartment doors, claiming to be the police. Joseph Cohen, a forester, opened the door.

The terrorists killed him and his seven-month pregnant wife, along with his 4-year-old son, Eliyahu, and wounded his 5-year-old daughter, Miriam.

From there it was on to the school where over a hundred high school students were settling down after a field trip. Some escaped, but the rest were taken hostage. A fuller account of this incident is in my previous book "Compulsion To Kill."

On March 11th, 1978 was another mass killing of children known locally as The Coastal Road Massacre. Eleven Islamic terrorists landed on a beach below a main road in Southern Israel. They first shot up a taxi and then hijacked a passing bus that was on an outing for employees of the bus company and their families. Using them as human shields, the terrorists then began shooting up passing cars, occasionally throwing grenades. The attack took place too deep inside Israel for military units to be in place to stop it. Instead, it was left to a few dozen traffic cops armed only with handguns, to set up a barricade and exchange fire with the attackers. One of the passengers managed to overpower a terrorist and get his gun. He then shot two of them. The remaining terrorists panicked and committed suicide after setting the bus on fire.

Reporters reaching the scene described the horror. "A child aged seven or eight was lying on the asphalt, a bullet hole in its head." Parents lost their children. And children lost their parents. Among the dead was a 5 year old along with his father. Habib Ankwa, who had volunteered to serve as a translator and mediator for the terrorists, was shot in the stomach when their plans were thwarted.

Along with him died his 10-year-old son Yitzchak and his 2-year-old daughter Galit. With the family, died 6-year-old Liat Gal- On, 5-year-old Naama Hadani, who was killed in her mother's arms, 6-year-old Yoav Meshkel and 9-year-old Mordechai Zit. Also killed were Joseph and Rebecca Hochman who were riding with their two sons, 3-year-old Ilan and 6-year-old Roi. While her husband bravely fought off the attackers, Rebecca was killed along with her two sons. Her husband survived but was wounded, resulting in the loss of the use of his legs. He was later awarded the medal of courage for his actions.

It is important to realize that the Palestine Authority does not see these events as terrorism or even unacceptable. Dozens of locations and events featured in massacres have been named after one of the terrorists Dalal Mughrabi a female whose act of heroism was dragging a baby back into the burning bus after its mother had managed to throw it clear.

Samir Kuntar became a hero of Lebanon. Syria's president Assad awarded him the Order of Merit, his dictatorship's highest honor. His brave achievement; Bludgeoning a 4-year-old girl to death. In Lebanon, Kuntar received a hero's welcome. Al Jazeera's Beirut office chief threw him a party and called him a Pan-Arab hero. Such behavior is unfathomable in civilized western cultures. The reason I mention these incidents is that it is important to realize the threat to our schoolchildren does not only come from deranged students. A second and far more deadly threat is out there.

Israel had learned a tragically hard lesson, but it was well learned. Today, armed teachers and guards are present at all schools, school trips and sporting events. There are no longer any gun free killing zones in Israel and the Islamic terrorists know it. The USA however still cling to the idea that passing a law stopping people from carrying guns in school will prevent a law breaker/killer from entering a school to shoot children.

The events at Columbine, Virginia Tech, and Sandy Hook have not blunted the liberal lawmakers from pursuing their insane political dogma. I feel sure that many, many more children will have to die before these lawmakers are booted out of office and common sense returns to the United States.

Chapter 2

Beslan, Slaughter of the Innocents

*"In this sad world of ours, sorrow comes to all;
and, to the young, it comes with bitterest agony,
because it takes them unawares. "*

Abraham Lincoln--December 23, 1862

Horrific as the events at Ma'alot were they paled
into insignificance compared to what happened in
a small town on the Chechnya / Russian border in
2004.

The town of Beslan is in many ways
unremarkable. Lying 900 miles south of Moscow
the community is largely agricultural and industry
and centered around a large vodka-producing
factory far from the pressures of politics and
warfare. It was to this town on September 1st 2004
that a group of terrorists from Chechnya came to
bring a whirlwind death and destruction, not
witnessed since the attacks of 9/11. The target of
these men was not military or even a civilian
airport. They headed straight for Beslan Middle
School where parents and children had gathered
for the traditional first day of term, the Day of
Knowledge.

The town had a population of just over 40,000 and several thousand were at the school, students, teachers, grandparents, and onlookers. Although Russian intelligence had received vague reports of a possible attack in the region, no specifics had been made and therefore one solitary soldier stood guard.

A Russian troop carrier and 3 other vehicles pulled up outside the school. The arrival did not cause any concern. The Russian military were not an uncommon sight in Beslan and since the town was close to the Chechnyan border, the sight of them was probably re-assuring. Among the crowd outside the school were 49 other terrorists who waited and watched. They were the eyes and ears of the assault team.

At a given moment the armed terrorists leapt from the vehicles armed with AK 47 semi automatic rifles and grenades, sniper rifles and explosives. They were immediately engaged by the armed guard and a solitary police officer in the crowd who drew his sidearm, both men fired, killing one terrorist before being cut down by a hail of gunfire. With all opposition now disposed of the terrorists then surrounded the crowd forcing them at gunpoint into the school and eventually into the school gymnasium, dividing them into two groups.

About 40 % of the crowd managed to break free from the gunmen and escape, the rest were herded inside and the doors barricaded.

By 9.05 AM the school was surrounded by police. Inside up to 50 fanatical terrorists were holding 1,181 hostages, most of whom were children. The crowd were stunned and could not understand what was happening and why. One father approached the school to ascertain the condition of the children. The terrorists immediately shot him dead, dragging his body inside. Such examples were the norm in the first few minutes of the siege. One man inside the building tried to calm the children and restore calm. This was the last thing the terrorists wanted. One walked up to him, put a gun to his head, and executed him in front of the screaming children.

Almost immediately the terrorists began the murder and rape that was to categorize this incident. Hostages were shot at random while the killers stripped and raped some girls in front of their parents. Other hostages were taken upstairs and repeatedly assaulted. The victims were aged 8 to 10 years.

As the screaming and gunfire intensified, those outside the school could not have imagined the scenes of horror cruelty taking place inside.

Calls went out for military assistance and in particular, to two elite anti- terrorist units, code named Alpha and Vympel, who were dispatched. These brave men would play a pivotal role in ending the siege, many paying the ultimate price for doing so.

Inside the school the situation became grimmer by the minute. The gunmen had brought explosives and other equipment with them. They had also learned from the earlier terrorist incident at the Nord -Orst theatre in Moscow (which was ended by a gas attack) and were equipped with gas masks. Explosives were draped around the school and wired up to the hostages. While the older children and men were forced at gunpoint to build barricades against the expected assault from the Russian forces. When the barricades were complete the older children and men were singled out, lined up against a wall and shot, their bodies being thrown from an upstairs window. The terrorists were aware that in school sieges in Columbine and Virginia Tech, some students had tackled the shooters. To prevent this they simply removed anyone deemed old or big enough to pose a risk.

Of course this siege was not carried out for any reason of forcing concessions or entering into negotiations. This was the new type of terrorism.

It was designed to spread horror, fear and dread among the population. This strategy, devised by the twisted mind of Osama Bin Laden was clearly illustrated on 9/11.

Above, a makeshift shrine at the burned out classroom, below Special Forces rescue the survivors. All images public domain.

The terrorists who attacked the school that day were not all Chechen they included Ingush, Arabs and North Africans. All were Islamic fundamentalists and among the group were two women wearing explosive suicide vests. The horrific details of the treatment of the children during the siege, I feel would be too graphic for me to repeat in this book and may detract from the core points I am trying to make. However, I do heartily recommend the reader to seek out the book *"Terror at Beslan" by John Giduck Archangel Group Inc.* This book gives a stark uncompromising view of the background and aftermath of the siege. As well as a minute by minute account of the event.

The surviving hostages reported after the event that the terrorists had made no attempt to hide their faces and had made it plain they expected to die. The situation was grim and the Russian forces outside knew it but were reluctant to move without orders. This changed when two bombs detonated in the gymnasium, blowing bodies in all directions; the result was the Russian troops outside immediately opened fire without direct orders and moved in.
As they did so they were engaged by terrorists firing from upstairs windows.

Specialist sniper teams positioned by the elite units engaged these gunmen and armed citizens in the crowd also joined the firefight, laying down a hail of gunfire at the windows forcing the terrorist to take cover. Specialist team Vympel stormed the main school building blowing holes in the walls to avoid triggering booby trapped doors and windows. Once inside they shepherded children to the holes and out of the building.

The enraged terrorists tried to mow them down as they fled across the playground. The terrorists had long planned for this attack and were well prepared. They had an easy time while shooting helpless children, but now they faced a crack team of elite commandos who could shoot back. Vympel team moved rapidly through the classrooms spraying the ceilings of each room with automatic fire and quickly eliminating every terrorist as they cowered under falling debris from the ceilings.

As both Vympel and Alpha teams moved through the building while the terrorists tried to fall back and regroup. They were ruthlessly cut down with no attempt at taking prisoners.

These troops had seen the slaughter and torture of these helpless children first hand, they were out to ensure that not one terrorist survived. In this they appeared to be almost totally successful.

It is however likely that some terrorists did escape in the confusion. It is still unknown exactly how many terrorist took part. What is known however is the sickening death toll which was 338 dead and 700 wounded which included 161 children.

Of course Beslan terrorists did make demands as did the 9/11 highjackers, but these demands were purely a feint designed to delay and counter offensive while plans were put into effect to kill as many people as possible. This mass murder concept was not immediately realized by the authorities. At Beslan, much time was wasted while various police and military commanders debated and argued as to how to proceed. Should similar disorganization occur in the USA at a similar event, the death toll will likely be even higher. So! Is that likely?

During the closing days of the Iraq war, US Special Forces raided a compound of one of the leaders of Saddam Hussein's Baath separatist party. The US forces recovered much valuable data. Including communications from the Terror mastermind Osama Bin laden. Also was a detailed set of plans of 5 Texas Elementary schools, detailing entrances, caretakers, and staff.

The question is, why would such details be of any use to an Iraqi official with ties to Osama Bin Laden?

The answer is almost too dark to contemplate.

The heartbreak of Beslan
Could these scenes be repeated here in the USA?

Chapter 3

What are they thinking of?

"Firearms stand next in importance to the Constitution itself. They are the American people's liberty teeth and keystone under independence ... From the hour the Pilgrims landed, to the present day, events, occurrences, and tendencies prove that to insure peace, security and happiness, the rifle and pistol are equally indispensable . . . the very atmosphere of firearms everywhere restrains evil interference - they deserve a place of honor with all that is good"

(George Washington)

The gun free zones as an idea born, purely and simply out of political ideology. Little consultation appears to have been done as to the practicality of implementing this policy with either the Police or public.
When I was a serving police officer in the UK, I recall a suggestion made by a police department (Not Hampshire) spokesman during a debate on stranded female motorists and the associated advice problems.

The suggestion was a female in this situation should display a sign in her vehicle stating LONE FEMALE STRANDED, which was deemed by the Police Department to be appropriate to attract attention! Well Dah! Yes I dare say it would.
The same logic seems to have been adopted by the administrations of New York City and California. (To name but two) The Brady group is the leading anti- gun organization in the USA today. It has been at the forefront of the campaign to undermine the Second Amendment and therefore can be seen by most logically minded people as anti-constitutional.

The United States is a free country, and its citizens, of course have a right to express any views they wish. Therefore, I in no way condemn the Brady group from putting its point of view. However I do reserve the right to fundamentally disagree with its views especially when, in my opinion those views put the lives of innocent people at risk.
Before we continue let us examine the Act in Question

The Gun Free School Zones Act 1990 states
(A) It shall be unlawful for any individual knowingly to possess a firearm that has moved in or that otherwise affects interstate or foreign commerce at a place that the individual knows, or has reasonable cause to believe, is a school zone.

(B) Subparagraph (A) does not apply to the possession of a firearm—
(i) on private property not part of school grounds;
(ii) if the individual possessing the firearm is licensed to do so by the State in which the school zone is located or a political subdivision of the State, and the law of the State or political subdivision requires that, before an individual obtains such a license, the law enforcement authorities of the State or political subdivision verify that the individual is qualified under law to receive the license;
(iii) that is— (I) not loaded; and (II) in a locked container, or a locked firearms rack that is on a motor vehicle;
(iv) by an individual for use in a program approved by a school in the school zone;
(v) by an individual in accordance with a contract entered into between a school in the school zone and the individual or an employer of the individual;
(vi) by a law enforcement officer acting in his or her official capacity; or
(vii) that is unloaded and is possessed by an individual while traversing school premises for the purpose of gaining access to public or private lands open to hunting, if the entry on school premises is authorized by school authorities.

(3) (A) Except as provided in subparagraph (B), it shall be unlawful for any person, knowingly or with reckless disregard for the safety of another, to discharge or attempt to discharge a firearm that has moved in or that otherwise affects interstate or foreign commerce at a place that the person knows is a school zone. (B) Subparagraph (A) does not apply to the discharge of a firearm—
(i) on private property not part of school grounds;
(ii) as part of a program approved by a school in the school zone, by an individual who is participating in the program;
(iii) by an individual in accordance with a contract entered into between a school in a school zone and the individual or an employer of the individual; or
(iv) by a law enforcement officer acting in his or her official capacity.
(4) Nothing in this subsection shall be construed as preempting or preventing a State or local government from enacting a statute establishing gun free school zones as provided in this subsection.

Definitions

Title 18 U.S.C. §921(25) The term "school zone" means— (A) in, or on the grounds of, a public, parochial or private school; or (B) within a distance of 1,000 feet from the grounds of a public, parochial or private school. (26) The term "school" means a school which provides elementary or secondary education, as determined under State law.

Penalty

Title 18 U.S.C Section 924(a) establishes the penalty for violating GFSZA:
Whoever violates the Act shall be fined not more than $5,000, imprisoned for not more than 5 years, or both. Notwithstanding any other provision of law, the term of imprisonment imposed under this paragraph shall not run concurrently with any other term of imprisonment imposed under any other provision of law.

Note: A conviction under the Gun Free Zones Act will cause an individual to become a "prohibited person" under the Gun Control Act 0f 1968. This will bar them from legally owning firearms for the rest of their life.
This fact is well known to both lawful citizens such as concealed weapon permit holders, and the criminal element. In effect, this law prevents anyone carrying a weapon within school districts, and other places.

The United States; it could be argued, is a nation founded on the use of firearms. The War of independence was sparked by the British army's attempt to disarm colonists who were deemed a threat. It is therefore not surprising that the founding fathers enshrined the right to keep and bear arms in the Nations Bill of Rights.

Back in the days of colonization, frontier families would have tarred and feathered any politician who dare suggest that they did not need guns for protection. Hostile Indians, Bears, wolves and marauding bands of outlaws, made a firearm not only desirable, but also essential for survival. The War of Independence, the Civil War, and two world wars are now behind us. America has forgotten the deep-rooted desire one gets of feeling safe in their homes, in their work and while going about their daily lives. The gun is now seen by some people in a totally different light.

Daily TV shows portray violence in many forms. Usually, the American West is now portrayed in a romantic heroic way. The noble sheriff outdraws the bad guy and sends him to boot hill, to the cheers of the townsfolk and his adoring lady. The honest cop defies corruption and indifference to arrest the criminals and make our lives safer. This is the vision of America that is portrayed to the rest of the world. In the UK while I was a police officer it was common to hear the comment, usually after a murder or shootout, that;

"We don't want guns here or it will become as bad as America."

When you asked, "well just how bad is America?" the response was usually, *"Well it's obvious, they all have guns and shoot up everything and everyone."*

Of course the more educated and reasonable among us, realize that this is a fundamental misunderstanding about gun ownership here, and of the American society in general.

The concept of the Second Amendment is misunderstood in Britain. The prime reason for this is that the United Kingdom does not have a Constitution. Its Laws come from Parliament and can, of course be repealed or amended at will. The concept therefore of a god given right is totally alien to the British lawmaker.

It was not always so. When the first gun control Act was introduced in the UK in 1920 the then Home Secretary assured the British public that the Act would in no way effect the right of law abiding citizens to defend themselves. That changed in 1937 when a new act deleted self-defense from the allowable reasons to own a firearm. The progression to a total ban is covered more fully in my book *'Debarred the Use of Arms", Outskirts Press, 2012*. But suffice it to say that the path to a total ban was then clear.

In the USA events have not mirrored the UK, primarily due to the Second Amendment. And the steadfast defense of the Constitution by groups such as The National Rifle Association.

That has not deterred the anti- gun politicians such as New York's Mayor Michael Bloomberg, whose disregard of the second amendment and persecution of gun owners is the stuff of legends.

The simple bumper sticker;
"When guns are outlawed only outlaws will have guns," is more than just a snappy slogan, it is a simple statement of the view of the pro gun lobby and the NRA. Most studies both here and internationally support the view that States and even Nations with strict gun control also have the highest rates of violent crime. The obvious conclusion to this fact is that, when faced with the possibility of victims being able to fight back and use deadly force in doing so, the criminal is less likely to attack a victim. They will simply choose another victim. The ideal place for the criminal to find such a victim has been provided by the authorities. The Gun Free Zones, where they can stalk their victims without fear of retaliation. When the possibility of resistance is removed, those criminals are more likely to attack.

In December 2012 the Libertarian Party issued the following statement on its decisions to campaign for the abolition of the Gun Free Zones.

The Libertarian Party said today the focus should be on ending the prohibition of self-defense in schools.

"We've created a 'gun-free zone,' a killing zone, for the sickest criminals on the face of the Earth," said R. Lee Wrights, vice-chair of the Libertarian Party. *"We've given them an open killing field, and <u>we've made the children of this country the victims.</u>"*
Wrights argued that the presence of guns on campus would be a strong deterrent: "They're not going to walk into a police station, and why not? Because that's where the guns are," he said.
The Federal Gun Free Schools Zone Act prohibits carrying firearms on school grounds in most cases. Without that law, the party argued, adults on campus could have been armed and ready to defend themselves and the children in the case of an attacker.
"We must stop blinding ourselves to the obvious: Most of these mass killings are happening at schools where self-defense is prohibited," said Carla Howell, executive director of the Libertarian Party. "Gun prohibition sets the stage for the slaughter of innocent children. We must repeal these anti-self-defense laws now to minimize the likelihood they will occur in the future and to the limit the damage done when they do."
The party noted that at this month's mall shooting in Portland, Ore., the gunman took his own life minutes after being confronted by a shopper carrying a concealed weapon.

A 2012 church shooting in Aurora, Colo., was stopped by a member of the congregation carrying a gun. A 2009 workplace shooting in Houston was halted by two co-workers who carried concealed handguns. And on and on.

Libertarians also note the post-9/11 prohibition on pilots carrying guns in the cockpit, a ban recently lifted when Congress acknowledged that the pilots would be better able to stop hijackers if armed.

"You can't depend on somebody else to take care of your own life for you," Wrights said. "It's too precious to put it into the hands of somebody else, particularly when the seconds count."

The Libertarian Party platform on self-defense states: "The only legitimate use of force is in defense of individual rights — life, liberty, and justly acquired property — against aggression. This right inheres in the individual, who may agree to be aided by any other individual or group. We affirm the individual right recognized by the Second Amendment to keep and bear arms, and oppose the prosecution of individuals for exercising their rights of self-defense. We oppose all laws at any level of government requiring registration of, or restricting, the ownership, manufacture, or transfer or sale of firearms or ammunition. It's impossible to imagine the depths of despair and grief that the victims' families are experiencing right now, said Geoffrey J. Neale, Chair of the Libertarian National Committee.

"Our hearts go out to every one of them."

Powerful stuff for a political party, well above the Republican view, but was anyone listening?
The party received the most votes in its history in the 2012 presidential contest: 1,272,105 cast for former New Mexico Gov. Gary Johnson. Those were more than double the 2008 total, and more than triple the party's 2004 count.

Of course the Libertarian party is some way from being able to form an effective government, but the surge in support must be worrying for the establishment. Politicians' main concern is getting votes and to do that they must connect with the people. Support for the second amendment is rising, NRA membership has soared, and gun sales are up to unprecedented levels. The result has left the anti- gunners off guard. The president and notable gun control advocates are quickly asserting that they too believe in the Second Amendment and the right to self-defense, however they struggle to explain why they are trying to restrict gun ownership for the US law-abiding public, but have no answer to keeping guns out of the hands of the criminal.

Of course, the Brady group and its supporters have a different interpretation on the figures. Despite the high body counts in high gun control cities, they insist on the logic that removing guns from the public will reduce gun crime.

Of course this would be true if all guns were eliminated and no one; Criminal, Citizen or Police officer carried guns. It is certain that in such a utopia, gun crime would diminish. Violent crime, well! That's another story.

But just as you cannot UN-invent the wheel to cure car accidents, then you cannot UN-invent the gun to cure gun crime. This simple truth will of course not prevent the anti groups from trying. When such ideas are put into Law, Gun Free Zones become Killing Zones.

Chapter 4

Another Indian Massacre

"The dumber people think you are, the most surprised they're going to be when you kill them."

William Clayton

In northern Minnesota close to the town of Bemidji lies the Red Lake Chippewa Reservation, home to some 5,000 Native Americans live on this vast, flat plain of isolation. Forty percent of the population is unemployed, most live in poverty, and both the number of gangs formed and the amount of drugs and alcohol consumed have been rising. On March 21, 2005 this reservation was the scene of another mass shooting. Ironically, it not as well covered as Columbine or Virginia Tech. Was this reflection on the casualties or just on the fact that what happens on what used to be called an Indian Reservation is not news worthy.

Jeff Weise was a 16-year-old Native American of the Chippewa tribe. Weise was a young man with a troubled history. His father had died in a stand off with police when he was 8 years old.

And he was raised by his grandmother, after his mother who had remarried was left wheelchair bound following a car accident. More domestic upheaval followed when his grandmother separated from her husband

Who was Jeff's grandfather who was a law enforcement officer with the reservations tribal Police.

On the day of the shooting, Weise collected a .22 caliber pistol from his bedroom and went into the room of his grandfather Daryl Allen Lussier, age 58 and shot him as he was sleeping; he shot him two times in the head and ten times in the chest. According to Weise's friends, the teenager may have had the gun for as long as a year. He took Lussier's two police-issue weapons, a .40 caliber Glock model 23 semi automatic pistol, and a Remington 870 12 gauge pump action, a gun belt and a bulletproof vest. He then fatally shot his Grandfathers girlfriend Michelle Leigh Sigana, age 31, two times in the head, as she was carrying laundry up the stairs.

Weise then drove his grandfather's police cruiser to the Red Lake Senior High School in Red Lake on the reservation. As he entered the school through the main entrance, he encountered two unarmed security guards who were manning a metal detector.

Weise shot and killed Derrick Brun, while the other security guard escaped without injury. Weise was now free to walk through the gun free zone school. Like others before and since, he was no doubt secure in the knowledge that he would meet no armed opposition. He went into the main corridor of the school.

He began shooting into an English classroom, killing three students and one teacher, and wounding three students. Ashley Lajeunesse said that Chase Lussier (no direct relation to Daryl Lussier) sheltered her, and was one of those shot by Weise.

Jeffrey May, a 16-year-old sophomore, tried to wrestle Weise inside the classroom, and managed to stab him in the stomach with a pencil, the diversion did allow other students to flee the classroom to safety. Enraged, Weise shot May two times in the neck and once in the jaw, leaving him seriously injured, though he did recover.

Witnesses said Weise smiled as he was shooting at people. One witness said that Weise asked a student if he believed in God. This may have been a reference to a widely publicized exchange between one of the shooters and a student during the 1999 Columbine shooting.

At around 2:52 p.m., Weise returned to the main entrance, where he killed two students and wounded two others. The police had arrived quickly and engaged him with gunfire. The shoot-out lasted for about four minutes. None of the officers were hit, but police bullets found their mark. Weise was hit in the abdomen and right arm, staggering away from the shoot out he retreated to a vacant classroom. As the Officers closed in, he leaned against a wall, put the shotgun barrel to his chin, and fired, killing himself instantly.
The shooting rampage had lasted 10 minutes, in which Jeff Weise killed a total nine people, 1 security guard, a teacher and five students, in addition to his Grandfather and his Grandfathers' girlfriend.

The Bemidji shooting was not too well reported but as with the other school shootings the killer fitted the profile of so many others. (*See "Compulsion to Kill" by Steve Challis, Amazon*)

Chapter 5

A Dark night indeed

"Every one of these places where terrible massacres had taken place, was a place where guns weren't allowed. Does anyone see a pattern here? So if guns are the problem, as the women across the mall assert, why haven't we seen any of these terrible mass shootings at NRA conventions, or skeet and trap shoots, or the dreaded gun show...places where there are perhaps thousands of guns in the hands of as many law abiding citizens who believe in their second amendment rights, if guns are the problem, someone explain this to me."

By Suzanna Gratia Hupp
"From Luby's to the legislature" Privateer Publications

The killing sprees in the federal mandated Gun Free zones were not confined to schools. The City of Aurora, Colorado is a sprawling township on the outskirts of Denver. Founded in the 1880s, it has little to put it on the map.

That all changed on July 22nd 2012. The Century 16 cinema complex at Aurora, Colorado was packed on the evening of Friday July 20th for the premiere of the new Batman movie "The Dark night."

Outside in the car park a figure walked purposely towards a wedged open fire exit. He was dressed in black and wore a military gas mask, load bearing vest, military ballistic helmet, bullet resistant leggings, throat protector, groin protector, and tactical gloves. He was carrying Remington 870 tactical shotgun and Smith and Wesson M& P 15 semi -automatic rifle fitted with a 100 round drum magazine.

Under any other circumstances this would have raised considerable alarm but the few in the audience considered the masked figure a threat. He appeared to be simply wearing a costume, like many other audience members who had dressed up for the screening. Others believed this was some sort of publicity stunt, or thought that he was part of a special effects installation set up for the film's premiere by the studio or theater management. In any event, little or no attention was paid to him. The action had reached full volume on the screen when this illusion was shattered. The gunman suddenly threw a canister emitting a gas or smoke.

This exploded, filling the air with acrid smoke which all but obscured the audience members' vision, making their throats and skin itch, and causing eye irritation. Coughing and screams filled the theatre as he then fired the shotgun, first at the ceiling and then at the audience. Dropping the shotgun, the gunman then opened fire with the M&P which fortunately, malfunctioned after reportedly firing fewer than 30 of the 100 rounds. This is common fault with this type of after market accessory, and the reason why most professionals' and instructors would not buy them.

Finally, he fired a Glock model 22 handgun. He shot first to the back of the room, and then toward people in the aisles. Some bullets passed through the wall and hit people in the adjacent theater, # 8, which was screening the same film. By this time the cinema was a bloodbath with the screams of the wounded and dying mixing with ringing of the cinemas auditorium smoke alarms.

After his murderous rampage, the killer walked out of into the car park and meekly surrendered to attending police officers, bizarrely announcing *"I am the Joker,"* an apparent reference to one of Batman's literary enemies.

The killer was 24-year-old James Holmes. He was a loner, a man who was virtually at war with everyone.

He had moved to Aurora to study at the University, a bright student who was studying neurology. But this bright career was on a spiral slope. Having recently broken up with his girlfriend, James started skipping lectures. The University had both counselors, and resident psychiatrists, and while as a student, James had taken up their services. However things deteriorated and James finally dropped out of his course.

James' world was now one of alternative reality. He was becoming more and more engrossed in video games. These games pitted him against zombies, aliens, and modern despotic armies. Behind the doors of his student apartment James also had another secret. He was buying guns, real guns and stockpiling ammunition. Holmes was a ticking time bomb and time had run out.
Aurora is a city with 7 cinemas, all showing the latest blockbusters and on a Friday night in July, most were premiering the new Batman film the "The Dark Knight."

The film had been much anticipated and many cinemagoers wore batman related outfits.
One of these was the cinemas was the Century 16 at 14300 East Alameda Avenue. It differed from the others in one respect. Century 16 was a gun free zone. The owners had posted notices that no weapons were allowed inside. This had two direct effects.

One, it gave certified concealed carry permit holders a warning that their custom was unwelcome, leading those people desiring to see the film to choose one of the other theaters. Secondly, and perhaps more importantly, it gave assurances to anyone looking to commit and armed crime a notice that there would be no armed opposition.

According to mapquest.com and movies.com, there were seven movie theaters showing "The Dark Knight Rises" on July 20th 2012, within 20 minutes of the killer's apartment, situated at 1690 Paris St, Aurora, Colorado. At a distance of a 4 miles and 8-minute car ride, the 'Cinemark Century Theater' wasn't the closest. Another theater was only 1.2 miles (3 minutes) away. There was also a theater just slightly further away, 10 minutes. It is the "home of Colorado's largest auditorium." The potentially huge audience ought to have been attractive to someone trying to kill as many people as possible. Four other theaters were 18 minutes, two at 19 minutes, and 20 minutes away. But all of those theaters allowed permitted concealed handguns.

So why would a mass shooter pick a place that bans guns?

The answer should be obvious, though it apparently was not so clear to the media, that disarming law-abiding citizens leaves them as vulnerable as sitting ducks when faced with an armed madman. Holmes knew that it was extremely unlikely that anyone in the cinema would oppose him. So! If there had been an armed cinemagoer in the cinema, could it have made a difference?

Well to answer that question let us look at the overall situation. Firearms instructor Monty Simao did this and made the following observations via a LinkedIn blog he posted shortly after the attack.

Picture sitting with your wife (or family) 2/3rds of the way back and center in the theater. The shooter is in the front. In order for you to take him out, you only have two choices:
1) The first is to take the shot from where you are seated. The benefits is that you can stay partially concealed behind the seats and it is a quicker solution. The disadvantages are "no shoots" getting in the way, distance to threat, and the fact that with distance you would probably go for center mass only to have your bullets stopped by body armor and now his attention is on YOU and the storm of lead coming your way hopefully doesn't find your wife.

Your follow-up shots for the head or pelvis would be considerably more difficult and for those of you who are carrying small .380s as your primary - shame on you!

2) Option two is to assault the position (get out of the kill zone). The shooter is at a tactical advantage. There are only two ways to physically get at him and that is up one of the two aisles that lead to the front of the theater. With the amphitheater shape, there is little concealment moving up the aisles, meaning that you are exposed and either moving low-n-slow or quickly. Your movement will catch his eye and a storm of lead. If you move up the closer aisle you have essentially put yourself into a fatal funnel, which he can easily cover with a minor pivot of his body.

From the above observations you can readily see that the situation is far from straightforward. It depends on a number of factors. The position that the armed citizen is in as relation to the shooter is a factor. There is also, the likelihood of hitting a bystander and the training to remain calm and steadily focused in such a situation. The Armed Citizen will have to be sure that the incident war rents a deadly force response. Remember this was the premier of a much-hyped film. Many attendees were dressed in costumes and it is well known that some cinema managements may perform stunts to promote films.

So! A concealed carry permit holder would not necessarily have been brought to a high sense of alert. Holmes timed his attack to occur when the action on the screen was intense, and most attendees would not be looking at him.
Therefore the first indication that something was wrong would come when the smoke grenades exploded and Holmes fired the first blast from his shotgun.

If the concealed carry holder had been seated close to Holmes he may have been able to draw and fire his gun within a 3 to 5 second window. That may have been enough; a hit in the face or head area would have incapacitated the shooter. A center mass or chest shot would have struck somewhere on the load bearing vest he was wearing. This vest is not bulletproof but in a darkened cinema, would that be obvious. Speaking for myself, I would take 5 to 10 seconds to evaluate the situation, to estimate the range, clothing that the perpetrator was wearing, the type of vest, and the type of firepower he was deploying. Add to this the scenes of utter pandemonium around, the screaming and panic flight of cinemagoers. The chance of another armed citizen being present and firing at the first man he sees with a gun, such as you is minimal, at best!
All told, the chances of an armed citizen or off duty officer being able to stop the threat are questionable, maybe no more than 30%.

However, we do have an example of what can happen when armed guards are present at a cinema when a shooter opens fire.

On Sunday, December 16, 2012 is a man at a similar movie theatre in San Antonio, Texas, for the sole purpose of killing his ex-girlfriend, because she had broken up with him. The gunman, 19-year-old Jesus Manuel Garcia, apparently did not complete his task. He opened fire at her in the theater restaurant which caused mass panic. People began running for cover and rushing towards exits, At least two people were wounded before the shooter went into the theatre where he encountered an off duty Bexar County Sheriffs officer, Sergeant Lisa Castellano was working there. She pursued the gunman who retreated into the men's room where Sgt. Castellano shot him several times causing him to drop his gun. The shooter had been stopped in his tracks by an armed officer who was in the right place at the right time. Needless to say, there was little or no reporting of this incident from the anti- gun media.

However the opportunity of armed intervention was denied to the helpless cinema audience in Aurora that night. The management of which had ensured they were unable to defend themselves. Cinema 16 was not made a gun free zone by the Government, the State nor even city ordinances. It was given that status by its owners.

In my opinion, they must bear the responsibility for that decision, and consequently blood is on their hands as well as those of the killer James Holmes.

Accused killer James Holmes at his initial Court appearance following the shootings

Chapter 6

Horror of the School Shootings

As a community, you've inspired us, Newtown. In the face of indescribable violence, in the face of unconscionable evil, you've looked out for each other. You've cared for one another. And you've loved one another. This is how Newtown will be remembered, and with time and God's grace, that love will see you through.

President Barack Obama
Dec 16, 2012
Newtown, Ct

The Amish were formed in 1693, and were born out of a breakaway faction of the Mennonites facing persecution from Catholic and Protestant Christians. Amish in large numbers eagerly took up William Penn's offer of religious freedom in the American colony of Pennsylvania. Immigration to Pennsylvania began in 1727 and continued in earnest through 1770, the settlement being concentrated in the Lancaster County area. From that time their numbers have grown to around 100,000. In the United States, the Amish are looked on as a quaint throwback to the days of the colonists and Quaker communities.

The sight of their horse drawn buggies and women wearing puritan dress are a big draw for photographers, though they dislike being photographed. They are a reminder to all Americans of their roots and deeply religious, with a set of morals that would put most Americans to shame. It is hard to believe that anyone would wish these people harm. However, on October 2nd 2006 in Lancaster County, Pennsylvania, a shooting occurred in a schoolhouse that seemed to defy all logic.

The incident occurred at the West Nickel Mines School, a one-room schoolhouse in the Old Order Amish community of Nickel Mines, a village in Bart Township. A local man with no connection to the community, Charles Carl Roberts IV, entered the schoolhouse armed with a Springfield XD 9mm handgun, a Browning 12 gauge pump action shotgun and a Ruger 30-06 bolt action rifle. He took the class and their teacher hostage. In addition to the weapons, Roberts carried about 600 rounds of ammunition, a number of cans of black powder (Gunpowder), a stun gun and, two knives, He also brought a change of clothes, an apparent truss board, and a box containing tools, screws bolts, and tape. He used 2x6 and 2x4 boards with eyebolts and flex ties to barricade the school doors before turning to the hostages. He bound their arms and legs before ordering them to line up against the chalkboard.

He then released the 15 male students present, along with a pregnant woman and three parents with infants.

The remaining 10 female students he kept inside the schoolhouse. The schoolteacher, who managed to escape, contacted the police. At approximately 10:36 a.m. the first police officers arrived and attempted (unsuccessfully) to communicate with Roberts using the PA system on their Cruisers. Roberts did not respond to them directly but called 911 and told the dispatchers that if police didn't get off the "property," he would kill the hostages. At approximately 11:07 a.m., Roberts began shooting the victims. State troopers immediately approached. Most of the girls were shot "execution style" in the back of the head. The ages of the victims ranged from six to thirteen. As the first trooper in line reached a window, the shooting abruptly stopped. Roberts had committed suicide. It took the troopers about two and a half minutes to break into the school to assist those children who were not killed instantly. Inside the school, Ballenger said, "there was not one desk, not one chair, in the whole schoolroom that was not splattered with either blood or glass. There were bullet holes everywhere, everywhere."

Janice Ballenger, deputy coroner in Lancaster County, Pennsylvania, told The Washington Post in an interview that she counted at least two dozen bullet wounds in one child alone before the stress proved too much and she asked a colleague to continue for her.

Following the shooting there was an unexpected turn of events. The Amish community reached out to the family of the killer and stated publically they had no animosity towards them and not even the Killer himself. The community elders also warned the younger members of the society to put aide any feelings of anger or revenge against the Roberts family. Such Christian values are rare following a killing of this magnitude. Despite leaving several bizarre suicide notes and some strange call to his wife, made from the schoolhouse, no motive has ever been established to account for Roberts's murderous rampage.

However one fact is very clear, one that links this shooting to others carried out in the USA and elsewhere. The school and its community were a gun free zone.

Not by legal statute, the peaceful status of the Amish was well known and even Police officers respect their views against guns. No! The Gun free zone is a self-imposed one. The gunmen who stalk these zones are inherently evil.

They have scant regard for their victims and specifically target gun free zones, because they offer the highest potential body count.
How many more children will be sacrificed by the misguided and dangerous policies of politicians who continually try and increase the number of gun free killing zones they control.

Tasso de Silveira.
On the morning of April 7, 2011, a 24-year-old man named Wellington Oliveira walked into Tasso de Silveira Municipal School, which is an elementary school in Realengo on the western fringe of the city of Rio de Janeiro, Brazil. After gaining access to the school, Oliveira, who was a former student, entered an 8th grade classroom. Oliveira was initially very polite to the students and saluted the children, but then without warning he opened fire on the class with two revolvers, a .38-caliber and a .32-caliber. Oliveira specifically targeted girls and shot boys only to immobilize them. He murdered 12 students, ten of them being female.

During the initial assault, a injured student who had escaped the carnage ran up to police officer Marcio Alves and blurted out what was happening. Officer Alves rushed to the school. He ran upstairs to the first and second floors, but found no sign of the killer. He confronted the heavily armed Oliveira on his way to the third floor.

Alves drew his sidearm and told Oliveira to stop. The warning was ignored. The Officer then shot him in the leg and stomach. Oliveira fell to the ground and shot himself dead before he could be arrested.

The school shooting was the first of its kind in Brazil. It was revealed that the suspect, Wellington Oliveira, was badly bullied in school and called strange.

His classmates used to call him "Sherman" (an allusion to a character from American Pie), as well as "suingue" (swing), because he had a limp leg. Two days before the shooting spree, Wellington Oliveira had made a video in which he said
"The struggle for which many brothers died in the past, and for which I will die, is not solely because of what is known as bullying. Our fight is against cruel people, cowards, who take advantage of the kindness, the weakness of people unable to defend themselves."
It was clear that Oliveira was a delusional individual that suffered from extreme rage and psychopathic tendencies.

Winnenden

On the morning of March 11, 2009, Kretschmer traveled to his former secondary school in Winnenden Germany, armed with a 9mm Beretta semi-automatic pistol, several 15-round magazines, and more than 200 rounds of ammunition. He was dressed in black combat clothing and had a gas mask. Upon entering the school, Kretschmer went toward a chemistry classroom full of 14 and 15-year-old students. He walked into the classroom and immediately opened fire.

Over the next two minutes, Kretschmer murdered eight girls, one boy, and three female teachers. He targeted females and shot his victims in the head. During the massacre, Kretschmer walked in and out of the chemistry classroom no less than three times. On the last visit he spoke his only words in the school: "Aren't you all dead yet?" The chilling quote shows the killers disregard for life and manic state. Immediately following the start of the attack, the school's headmaster broadcast a coded announcement saying, "Mrs. Koma is coming," which is amok spelled backwards. The message was a safety measure installed to alert the teachers of a school shooting. There was of course little they could do. German schools have no armed security either.

Two minutes after the rampage started, three armed police officers did arrive and entered the building, interrupting the attack. Kretschmer quickly fled the scene and killed a 56-year-old gardener (caretaker) of a nearby psychiatric hospital. He carjacked a vehicle driven by a man named Igor Wolf and ordered him to drive out of the area. While in the car, Wolf tried to calm the youngster asking Kretschmer why he murdered the children. The response was chilling, "For fun, because it is fun."

Kretschmer then continued, "Do you think we will find another school?" Wolf quickly changed the subject.

Realizing that he would almost certainly be the next victim Wolf steered the car toward a grass verge and following the impact he jumped from the vehicle and escaped.
Kretschmer then left the scene and entered a Volkswagen car showroom where he killed two more people, firing thirteen shots into each victim. Now Kretschmer really lost it. He left the building and started shooting all directions. Attending Police officers opened fire, hitting Kretschmer in the leg. As is usual in such cases, the killer then shot himself.

In the event, Tim Kretschmer killed 15 people. The school shooting, was at the time, the 5th most deadly in world history.

On the night before the attack, Kretschmer chatted on the internet about his intention to commit mass murder. He wrote; "No one sees my potential. I'm serious. I have weapons and I will go to my former school in the morning and have a proper barbecue. Maybe I'll get away. Listen out. You will hear of me tomorrow. Remember the place's name, Winnenden."

Chapter 7

The Tragedy of Sandy Hook

If one single incident of mass shooting in the USA stands out for its sheer brutality and shock effect it is that at a small elementary school in Connecticut called Sandy Hook.

What made Sandy Hook special was not the horrific slaughter of so many small innocent and trusting children. It was the almost indecent haste in which politicians and anti-gun groups exploited the tragedy to the fullest extent.
I saw the same vitriol in England after Dunblane incident. That incident led to the banning of most handguns there, and that in turn led to a massive increase in violent crime.

The National Rifle Association, following their usual practice kept silent on the incident, at least publically. Members and affiliated clubs were asked not to comment until the police had carried out initial enquiries and the families had the chance to grieve and bury their dead. It was a policy that was criticized by some, but it was one I was in complete agreement with.

The Sandy hook killer, 20-year-old Adam Lanza was a young man who clearly had problems.

He lived with his mother in a large house and had a lifestyle most would envy. Divorced from her husband who had provided a very generous settlement, Adam's mother was by most standards well off. She and her family moved to the Sandy Hook neighborhood about 1998, raising two sons with her husband Peter until the couple separated and divorced in 2008. With Ryan, Adam's brother, choosing to live with his father, Nancy was left to raise Adam alone. Adam was proving a difficult adolescent to live with. His mother was clearly troubled by her sons somewhat bizarre behavior. She had confided this to friends and on Facebook, but did not go into specifics. She also said Adam was on serious medication but did not elaborate. It is known that Nancy took Adam to see a psychiatrist but the reason has so far not been disclosed.

Far from being anti- gun, Nancy Lanza was aware of the consequences of being a well off divorcee living in a country location. She had purchased two handguns, 2 hunting rifles and an AR 15 Bushmaster (.223 semi- automatic rifle), and by all accounts knew how to use them. She had often told friends that she loved shooting at the Range with her sons, though investigators have been unable to confirm that.

The gun laws in Connecticut are some of the strictest in the USA.

They prevented Adam from purchasing a gun legally but had no effect on his desire to kill. Sometime overnight on December 14th to the 15th of 2012 Lanza made his fateful decision. He had tried and failed to obtain a weapon, and he had dark secrets that caused him to ensure the hard drive on his computer was totally destroyed. Police were unable to glean any information from the smashed computer, and Lanza did not leave any suicide note. So we can only speculate as to his mindset. Obviously there will be no trial and therefore no psychiatric testimony. Eventually the results of an enquiry will be known, but how much of it will be released, is anyone's guess.

In my book *"Compulsion to Kill,"* I profiled a number of serial killers and among those was Thomas Hamilton, who shot preschool toddlers and their teacher in a Scottish Kindergarten. Hamilton was a man who had a compulsive hatred of the members of the society he lived in and he blamed the police and many of the parents of his victims for his misfortunes. Killing their children was his way of exacting revenge; I believe the same psychotic drive motivated Adam Lanza. At 20 years old, Adam was too young to purchase a gun legally. Even if he was of age, he would hardly have been willing to wait the mandatory 2 weeks waiting period required by Connecticut law.

But Adam was aware that his mother owned guns, and due to her concerns about home invasions, these guns were not locked away. Of course, even if they were, it would have made no difference. Once he had made the decision to kill his sleeping mother he would have access to her keys. Just why he decided on Sandy Hook school for his bloody rampage is not clear. But like every other gun free zone, he knew that there would be no armed opposition.

Sometime early on that Friday Morning Adam walked into his mother's bedroom and shot her in the forehead with a .22 rifle which he then left on the bedroom floor. His mother was asleep and dressed in pajamas when he shot her.
The remoteness of the house meant that no one heard the shot.

Adam Lanza dressed in black cargo pants and top with a green military tactical vest in which he carried spare magazines for the AR 15. He left the house taking the AR 15 and two handguns, a Glock 10mm semi auto pistol and a Sig-Saur 9mm semi auto pistol. At this point he had already committed murder and theft, he then took his mothers car and drove to the school. Having committed 3 crimes already, the children's only hope was that this lawbreaker would respect the law on Sandy Hook being a gun free zone. Needless to say it was a forlorn hope.

Lanza arrived at the school and pulled up outside the main entrance, leaving the car and an Izhmash Canta 12 gauge shotgun on the rear seat. It is unsure if the shotgun was taken from the house by Lanza or if it was previously in the car. He approached the main door which was locked, in accordance with the schools security protocols. A burst of rapid fire from the AR 15 (.223-caliber Bushmaster XM15-E2S) he carried, destroyed the lock. Once inside, Lanza moved down the corridor to the principal's office.

Principal Dawn Hochsprung and the school psychologist Mary Sherlach were meeting with other faculty members when they heard the gunshots as Lanza entered the building. At that moment the schools intercom was activated. Hochsprung and Sherlach immediately left the room, rushed to the source of the sounds, and encountered and confronted Lanza. With no hesitation he shot and killed both women.
A nine-year-old boy who survived the massacre said he heard the shooter say: "Put your hands up!" and someone else say, "Don't shoot!", people yelling and many gunshots over the intercom as he, his classmates, and teacher took refuge in a closet in the school gymnasium.

Diane Day, a school therapist who was at the faculty meeting, heard screaming followed by more gunshots.

Natalie Hammond, lead teacher in the meeting room, pressed her body against the door to keep it closed. Lanza shot through the door, hitting her in her leg and arm. She was later treated at Danbury Hospital and recovered. The police reported that a second adult was wounded in the attack, but that individual was not identified.

In a first-grade classroom, Lauren Rousseau, a substitute teacher, was shot in the face and killed. Fifteen of the sixteen students in her class were killed; as Lanza poured continuous fire at the children. A six-year-old girl was the sole survivor. The girl's family pastor said that she survived the mass shooting by playing dead and remaining still until the building grew quiet, and she felt it was safe to leave. She ran from the school, covered in blood, and was the first child to escape the building. When she reached her mother, she said, "Mommy, I'm okay, but all my friends are dead." The child described the shooter as a very angry man.

The events in another first-grade classroom remain uncertain, with varying accounts attributed to the surviving children. Teacher Victoria Leigh Soto was reported to have attempted to hide several children in a closet and cupboards. As Lanza entered her classroom, Soto reportedly told him that the children were in the auditorium.

Several of the children then came out of their hiding place and tried to run for safety. Lanza immediately gunned them down. Soto then put herself between her students and the shooter in a vain attempt to save them, Lanza then fatally shot her. Six surviving children from Soto's class waited until the killer had left and crawled out of the cupboards and fled the school. They and a school bus driver took refuge at a nearby home. Anne Marie Murphy, a teacher's aide who worked with special-needs students, shielded six-year-old Dylan Hockley with her body, in a brave but futile attempt to protect him from Lanza's rampage. He was unmoved and the bullets killed them both. This one killing hit home to me personally very hard. I did not know Dylan or his parents, but he came originally from Eastleigh, my hometown in England. I wish that I or someone like me could have been there to stand between the mad dog and his victims, but there was no one. The gun free zone created by a misguided government had seen to that.

Paraprofessional Rachel D'Avino, who had only been employed at the school working with a special-needs student for a little more than one week, also died that day trying to protect her students.

School nurse Sally Cox, 60, hid under a desk in her office and described the door opening and seeing Lanza's boots and legs facing her desk from approximately 20 feet (6.1 m) away. He remained standing for a few seconds before turning around and leaving. She and school Secretary Barbara Halstead then hid in a first-aid supply closet for up to four hours, after calling 911. School Custodian Rick Thorne ran through hallways, alerting classrooms.

First grade teacher Kaitlin Roig, age 29, hid 14 students in a bathroom and barricaded the door, telling them to be completely quiet to remain safe. School library staff Yvonne Cech and Maryann Jacob first hid 18 children in a part of the library the school used for lockdown in practice drills, but on discovering that one of the doors would not lock, had the children crawl into a storage room as Cech barricaded the door with a filing cabinet. Music teacher Maryrose Kristopik, 50, barricaded her fourth-graders in a tiny supply closet during the rampage.

Lanza arrived moments later, pounding and yelling, "Let me in," while the students in Kristopik's class quietly hid inside.

Two third graders, chosen as classroom helpers, were walking down the hallway to the office to deliver the morning attendance sheet as the shooting began. Teacher Abbey Clements pulled both children into her classroom, where they hid. Laura Feinstein, a reading specialist at the school, gathered two students from outside her classroom and hid with them under desks after they heard gunshots. Feinstein called the school office and attempted to call 9-1-1 but was unable to connect because her cell phone did not have reception. She hid with the children for approximately 40 minutes, before law enforcement came to lead them out of the room.

Lanza stopped shooting between 9:46 a.m. and 9:49 a.m., after firing a total of 154 rounds. He reloaded frequently during the shooting, sometimes firing only fifteen rounds from a thirty round magazine. He shot all of his victims multiple times, and at least one victim, six-year-old Noah Pozner, 11 times. He shot mostly in two first-grade classrooms near the entrance of the school, killing fourteen in one room and six in the other. The student victims were eight boys and twelve girls, between six and seven years of age, and the six adults were all women who worked at the school. Bullets were also found in at least three cars parked outside the school. Police later think that Lanza may have fired at them as they arrived, though there is no witness to confirm that.

Police were swift to arrive following the 911 calls. One officer entered and was spotted by Lanza. Having caused as much damage as he could, Lanza was in no mood to take on someone who could and would shoot back. Lanza dropped the AR 15 and killed himself with a shot to the front of the head from a Glock 9mm handgun. No police Officers fired any rounds during the incident.

In fact, when Police Officers entered the school they found only two weapons The AR 15 Bushmaster rifle and the 9mm Glock handgun that he used to take his own life. The classrooms were littered with spent .223 cases from the AR15. There were one hundred fifty four (154) cases in all. These gave mute testimony of the way the massacre progressed. The AR 15 takes a variety of magazine sizes, from 5 to 30 rounds. Police also discovered that the Bushmaster rifle was loaded with 14 rounds in its 30-round capacity magazine, plus one round in a chamber.

This was one of 10 of this firearm's 30-round capacity magazines at the scene, State's Attorney Stephen J. Sedensky III explained. More ammunition for the Glock and a Sig Sauer P226 (9 mm) handgun was also found. Three such magazines still contained 30 rounds. There were six more magazines nearby -- three of them were empty, while the others had 10, 11, or 13 live rounds in them.

"One-hundred-and-fifty-four spent .223 casings were recovered from the scene," the state's attorney wrote, indicating that Lanza had fired at least that many bullets, from what Connecticut authorities had described as an "assault-type rifle." Lanza found the door locked on arrival at the school. It was locked promptly at 0930 hours each morning. That means that the police response time was quite good, approximately 10-15 minutes. However no 911 calls were made until Lanza started shooting. Therefore the only possibility of anyone stopping Lanza would have been a police officer in the school at the time, or one of the staff having access to a gun.

Adam Lanza was a very disturbed individual. In my previous book "Compulsion to Kill" I identified 3 common traits that apply to the mass school shooting perpetrators. Adam Lanza fitted this profile exactly. It was no surprise. This young man suffered from a psychological disorder, he was a loner addicted to video games and felt society was plotting against him.
In addition to the items at the school, Police meticulously searched Lanza's home. The official Police report lists the following items that were seized.
1 Bag with 30 Winchester 12-gauge shotgun shells
1 can with .22 caliber and .45 caliber rounds
8 boxes of Winchester Wildcat .22 caliber rounds, 50 rounds per box

20 "Estate" 12-gauge shotgun shells

4 boxes of SB buckshot 12-gauge, 10 round per box

1 box of Lightfield 12-gauge slugs

1 box of 20 Prvi Partizan 303 British rifle cartridges

1 box of 20 Federal 303 British rifle cartridges

2 boxes of .22 long rifle Blazer rounds, 50 each box

1 box with numerous rounds of Winchester .45 caliber bullets

2 boxes of 50 rounds of PPU .45 caliber automatic

1 box of 20 rounds for Remington .223 caliber

3 boxes of Blazer 40 S&W, 50 rounds each

2 boxes of Winchester 5.56 mm, 20 rounds each

1 box of Magtech 45 ACP with 30 rounds

1 empty Box of SSA 5.56 mm

1 box of Fiocchi .45 auto with 48 rounds

80 rounds of CCI .22 long rifle

6 boxes of PMC .223 Remington, 20 rounds each

6 Winchester 9 pellet buckshot shells, 12-gauge

2 Remington 12-gauge slugs

3 Winchester .223 rifle rounds

31 .22 caliber rounds

2 boxes of Underwood 10 mm auto, each with 50 rounds

130 rounds of Lawman 9mm Luger

2 spent shell casings for Glock 10mm

1 empty box of Gold Dot 9mm Luger

2 empty boxes of Winchester 9mm Luger

1 box of Underwood 10mm auto with 34 rounds

1 box of 29 miscellaneous 9mm rounds
1 spent .22 shell casing
1 small plastic bag containing numerous .22 caliber rounds
1 tan bag with numerous Blazer .45 caliber rounds
1 box of Blazer .22 long rifle with 50 rounds
1 box PPU 303 British cartridges with 9 rounds
2 Winchester 9mm rounds
2 brass-colored shell casings
1 small caliber bullet (live round) labeled C
Magazines:
1 Promag 20-round 12-gauge drum magazine
1 MD Arms 20-round 12 gauge drum magazine
3 AGP Arms 12-gauge shotgun magazines
1 Surefire GunMag magazine with 8 rounds of Winchester 12-gauge, 9-pellet buckshot
2 AGP Arms 12-gauge shotgun magazines, taped together, each with 10 rounds of Winchester 9-pellet buckshot
2 empty Ram Line magazines for Ruger 10-22
1 AGP Arms Gen 2 12-gauge shotgun magazine with 10 rounds of Winchester 12-gauge, 9-pellet buckshot
1 clear plastic Ram Line magazine for an AR 15
1 magazine with 10 rounds of .223 bullets
Knives:
Metal bayonet
1 6-foot-10-inch wood-handled two-sided pole with a blade on one side and a spear on the other
1 Samurai sword with a 28-inch blade and sheath
1 Samurai sword with a 21-inch blade and a sheath

1 Samurai sword with a 13-inch blade and sheath
1 knife with a 12-inch blade and sheath
1 wooden-handle knife with a 7.5-inch blade and sheath
1 wooden-handle knife with a 10-inch blade
1 knife with a 5.5-inch blade and sheath
1 black-handled knife with a 7-inch blade and sheath
1 black rubber-handled knife with 9.5-inch blade and sheath
1 white and brown-handled knife with 5-inch blade and sheath
1 brown wood-handled knife with a 10.25-inch blade
1 Panther brown-handled folding knife with a 3.75-inch blade
1 small blue folding knife
Gear:
1 Volcanic .22 starter pistol with 5 live rounds and 1 expended round
Leightning L3 ear protection
Peltor earplugs
Simmons binoculars
Uncle Mike's Sidekick nylon holster
Box for vest accessories
Leather dual magazine holder
Black leather handgun holster
High Sierra fanny pack
Numerous paper targets
1 cardboard target
1 Bushnell sport view rifle scope

Plastic bag of miscellaneous parts
Safariland holster paperwork
Glock handgun manual
MD-20 20-round shotgun magazine manual
MD Arms V-Plug guide
Bushmaster XM15 and C15 instruction manual
Savage Arms bolt-action rifle manual
Glock paperwork
Miscellaneous:
Adam Lanza's National Rifle Association
certificate
Nancy Lanza's NRA certificate
Three photographs with images of what appears to
be a deceased human covered with plastic and
what appears to be blood
Holiday card with a check from Nancy Lanza to
Adam Lanza for purchase of C183 firearm
1 digital print of a child and various firearms
1 military-style uniform
Handwritten notes with addresses of local gun
shops
Receipts and emails documenting firearm and
ammunition supplies
Blue folder labeled "guns" with receipts and
paperwork
Paperwork titled "Connecticut Gun Exchange
Glock 20SF 10mm" dated 12-21-11
Sandy Hook report card for Adam Lanza
New York Times article on a 2008 shooting at
Northern Illinois University

Books:
"Look me in the Eye: My Life with Asperger's",
"Born on a Blue Day: Inside the Mind of an
Autistic Savant",
"NRA Guide to Basics of Pistol Shooting",
"Train Your Brain to Get Happy"
1 Seagate Barracuda 500GB hard drive, damaged
1 custom-built desktop computer, no hard drive
1 Microsoft Xbox with partially obliterated serial
number
One cotton swab of blood-like substance
1 tan sheet with blood-like substance
1 tan fitted sheet with blood-like substance
1 striped towel with blood-like substance
The list of items recovered at the school tells us
something also about Lanza's intentions.
1 Bushmaster .223 caliber model XM15 rifle with
a 30-round magazine
1 Glock 10mm handgun
1 9mm Sig Sauer P226 handgun
1 Saiga 12 shotgun with two magazines containing
70 rounds
10 30-round magazines, three of them emptied.

The grief of this Newtown officer is one of the
enduring images to come out of Sandy Hook.

Nancy Lanza, Adams mother became his first
victim, when she was shot while asleep on the
morning of the killings.

The shotgun was found in the back seat of the car that Lanza parked close to the school entrance. First reports from Gun ignorant reporters stated this was an AR 15 and this lead to the ridiculous conspiracy theories that the story was a hoax or a gun control designed conspiracy. This just added to the anguish of the victims parents and is another example of sensationalistic journalism at its worst. Unfortunately, they have learned little and in late March the largest newspaper in Iowa "The De Moines Register" published an interactive map showing schools with little or no security. The map was a gift to any budding killer looking to top Lanza's score. The paper took the page down after a barrage of complaints from worried parents but the damage may well have been done. Should another mass killing occur there, no doubt the newspaper will insist it was nothing to do with them and blame the gun used or the NRA. With such irresponsibility from our government and the media the next mass shooting is only a matter of time.

Of the list of items found in the home, I found some items of interest. The books on Autism and mental conditions related to a mental condition that Adam was reportedly suffering. They show Adams mother was researching her sons mental state.

The NRA certificates and book were of course jumped on by the Anti gun zealots as proof that the NRA in some way bore responsibility for the attack. In fact neither Adam nor his mother was NRA members.

The police did not elaborate on the certificates, but the book on basic pistol shooting gives us a strong clue. These books are exclusive to the NRA and are issued to students who attend and successfully complete an NRA basic Pistol course run by a certified instructor. Membership of the NRA is not required to attend one of there certified courses. NRA instructors who run such courses are required to submit reports to the NRA which should contain the names of the students. If the certificates are dated it would be a simple matter to cross check with the training department and see if the names show up.

Even if they do, it does not, in any way mean that the NRA instructor concerned could have foreseen that one of his students may become mentally disturbed at some time in the future. Any more than a doctor can guarantee his patient may not develop cancer later in life. As a certified NRA instructor myself I have run numerous basic pistol courses and passed out certificates to each successful student.

The guns and ammunition found at the home were neither illegal, nor excessive in any home that embraces gun ownership.

That is not to say that there are lessons to be learned here. Adam Lanza's mother clearly knew that her son was a risk. She was aware of his mental state and as a single mother wanted to interact with her son. By involving herself in his interest in guns she most likely felt she could steer him into adulthood. But it was a risky strategy. Keeping guns around without adequate security seems foolhardy, but we cannot know for certain if the guns were locked up or not. There was a gun safe in the house and the police found the guns unsecured. Did Lanza retrieve the guns from the safe that morning? Did he intend to kill a greater number of children? The extra ammunition and firepower he took to the school would certainly suggest so, but these questions are unlikely to be answered. The only persons who know for sure are both dead. And the Police have to try and gain answers from the evidence left behind.

The evidence does not show that gun laws would have prevented this tragedy. It is incomprehensible to me that with all the horror surrounding this incident that not one serious attempt was made to look at any law that could have prevented the incident.

Background checks on mentally disturbed individuals have been ruled out by the Obama administration. Controls on violent video games and media have similarly been dismissed. Even allowing armed guards or concealed carry holders in schools has been vetoed.

The Gun free zone chosen by Lanza was a perfect target for his purposes. His mad spree was stopped only by the arrival of the Police.

With the weapons he had with him and the extra ammunition carried, he expected to be able to carry on killing until he ran out of targets. This madness of creating these target zones and allowing mad men to use them to kill children has to stop.

The shock and horror of Sandy hook and its effect on the Nation cannot be over-emphasized. In my book *"Debarred the Use of Arms"* (outskirts press) which was published on March 4, 2012, I predicted that there would inevitably another mass shooting in a gun free zone in the USA in the near future. That shooting occurred as my follow up book *"Compulsion to Kill,"* was in final editing. I did consider delaying the books publication as the story unfolded. The decision to go ahead was a difficult one and was based solely on the subject matter which dealt with the mindset of the mass school killer.

I hope that my insights may help in preventing another such tragedy. The guns used by Adam Lanza were not illegally obtained. All were bought legally under Connecticut's already strict gun laws. A fact admitted by the State Governor Dannel Malloy, in a call for stricter gun laws he made the following statement on the 27th of March, 2013.

"We knew that these weapons were legally purchased under our current laws," Malloy said. "I don't know what more we can need to know before we take decisive action to prevent gun violence. The time to act is now."

I had also hoped that such a horrific incident may at last illustrate the insane policy of creating a gun free zone at the most vulnerable of our establishments, our schools. The fact that our Banks, Politicians, Hollywood Stars and of course our President are considered valuable enough to protect with Armed Security, but our Children are not considered worth the effort, is appalling. Instead we get the well-worn argument from the President and his supporters that it was the gun that was at fault, we must ban the guns, and all the killings would stop.

Off course, that does not mean that the President, Banks, or the Celebrities will have no guns. The Police, Security, and Hollywood will still be protecting them.

No it will be the American citizen who wants to protect himself and his family from the likes of Adam Lanza and won't be able to. Those are the people the gun ban will affect.

The criminals will of course reap the biggest reward, the elimination of any serious defense and the adoption of larger gun free killing zones to provide the killers with more targets/human shooting arcades. So what is the view of those directly involved in these shootings, the survivors? What do they believe? Well! You may think they would be anti-gun, and in fact some are. These are the ones that make the news. However there are survivors on the other side. I met one survivor in 2011, who took a course at our shooting school in Kentucky.

Below I have reprinted an open letter sent to President Obama from one of the survivors of Columbine. Which was published on the internet and is in the public domain?

"Mr. President,
As a student who was shot and wounded during the Columbine massacre, I have a few thoughts on the current gun debate. In regards to your gun control initiatives:
Universal Background Checks
First, a universal background check will have many devastating effects.

It will arguably have the opposite impact of what you propose. If adopted, criminals will know that they cannot pass a background check legally, so they will resort to other avenues. With the conditions being set by this initiative, it will create a large black market for weapons and will support more criminal activity and funnel additional money into the hands of thugs, criminals, and people who will do harm to American citizens.

Second, universal background checks will create a huge bureaucracy that will cost an enormous amount of taxpayers' dollars and will straddle us with more debt. We cannot afford it now, let alone create another function of government that will have a huge monthly bill attached to it.

Third, is a universal background check system possible without universal gun registration? If so, please define it for us. Universal registration can easily be used for universal confiscation. I am not at all implying that you, sir, would try such a measure, but we do need to think about our actions through the lens of time.

It is not impossible to think that a tyrant, to the likes of Mao, Castro, Che, Hitler, Stalin, Mussolini, and others, could possibly rise to power in America. It could be five, ten, twenty, or one hundred years from now — but future generations have the natural right to protect themselves from tyrannical government just as much as we currently do.

It is safe to assume that this liberty that our forefathers secured has been a thorn in the side of would-be tyrants ever since the Second Amendment was adopted.

Ban on Military-Style Assault Weapons

The evidence is very clear pertaining to the inadequacies of the assault weapons ban. It had little to no effect when it was in place from 1994 until 2004. It was during this time that I personally witnessed two fellow students murder twelve of my classmates and one teacher. The assault weapons ban did not deter these two murderers, nor did the other thirty-something laws that they broke.

Gun ownership is at an all time high. And although tragedies like Columbine and Newtown are exploited by ideologues and special-interest lobbying groups, crime is at an all time low. The people have spoken. Gun store shelves have been emptied. Gun shows are breaking attendance records. Gun manufacturers are sold out and back ordered. Shortages on ammo and firearms are countrywide. The American people have spoken and are telling you that our Second Amendment shall not be infringed.

10-Round Limit for Magazines

Virginia Tech was the site of the deadliest school shooting in U.S. history. Seung-Hui Cho used two of the smallest caliber handguns manufactured and a handful of ten round magazines.

There are no substantial facts that prove that limited magazines would make any difference at all.

Second, this is just another law that endangers law-abiding citizens. I've heard you ask, "Why does someone need 30 bullets to kill a deer?" Let me ask you this: Why would you prefer criminals to have the ability to out-gun law-abiding citizens? Under this policy, criminals will still have their 30-round magazines, but the average American will not. Whose side are you on?

Lastly, when did they government get into the business of regulating "needs?" This is yet another example of government overreaching and straying from its intended purpose.

Selling to Criminals

Mr. President, these are your words: "And finally, Congress needs to help, rather than hinder, law enforcement as it does its job. We should get tougher on people who buy guns with the express purpose of turning around and selling them to criminals. And we should severely punish anybody who helps them do this."

Why don't we start with Eric Holder and thoroughly investigate the Fast and Furious program?

Furthermore, the vast majority of these mass murderers bought their weapons legally and jumped through all the hoops — because they were determined to murder. Adding more hoops and red tape will not stop these types of people. It doesn't now — so what makes you think it will in the future? Criminals who cannot buy guns legally just resort to the black market.

Criminals and murderers will always find a way.

Critical Examination

Mr. President, in theory, your initiatives and proposals sound warm and fuzzy — but in reality they are far from what we need. Your initiatives seem to punish law-abiding American citizens and enable the murderers, thugs, and other lowlifes who wish to do harm to others.

Let me be clear: These ideas are the worst possible initiatives if you seriously care about saving lives and also upholding your oath of office. There is no dictate, law, or regulation that will stop bad things from happening — and you know that. Yet you continue to push the rhetoric. Why?

You said, "If we can save just one person it is worth it." Well here are a few ideas that will save more that one individual:

First, forget all of your current initiatives and 23 purposed executive orders. They will do nothing more than impede law-abiding citizens and breach the intent of the Constitution. Each initiative steals freedom, grants more power to an already-overreaching government, and empowers and enables criminals to run amok.

98

Second, press Congress to repeal the "Gun Free Zone Act." Don't allow America's teachers and students to be endangered one-day more. These parents and teachers have the natural right to defend themselves and not be looked at as criminals. There is no reason teachers must disarm themselves to perform their jobs. There is also no reason a parent or volunteer should be disarmed when they cross the school line.

This is your chance to correct history and restore liberty. This simple act of restoring freedom will deter would-be murderers and for those who try, they will be met with resistance. President, do the right thing, restore freedom, and save lives. Show the American people that you stand with them and not with thugs and criminals.

Respectfully,

Severely Concerned Citizen, Evan M. Todd"

Mr. Todd makes very valid points. Remember, he was shot in a school shooting, and lived to tell the tale. He knows far better than any politician, the reality of coming face to face with an armed killer in a gun free zone. We would do well to listen to him.

Chapter 8

God and Guns

But now, he who has a money bag, let him take it, and likewise a sack; and he who has no sword, let him sell his garment and buy one"

Jesus Christ (Luke. 22:36).

There is one other gun free zone area that many States adopt, though the criminals of course ignore such exemptions. Those zones are the churches and places of worship.

The idea of carrying a firearm into a house of worship is of course at odds with most Christian views.

The regulations are to say the least patchy. In Ohio, there is a State law that imposes a 4th degree felony if a church member with a concealed handgun license brings their firearm to church as a means of protection against such an attack. The law calls for him to be arrested and charged with a felony of the fourth degree, and a conviction would earn him up to $5,000 in fines and 18 months in prison.

That did not stop a shooting over the Easter weekend 2013, Richard Riddle, 52, was leaving the church on Hiawatha Street with his wife at about 1 p.m. when his son, 25-year-old Reshad Riddle, approached him and fired a single round from a handgun, instantly killing Richard, church associate pastor Sean Adams said.

About 150 parishioners were leaving the church in recessional. They ducked down at the sound of the gunshot, pushing their children and grandchildren under the pews as Reshad Riddle entered the church, still carrying the gun and yelling that the shooting was "the will of Allah. This is the will of God," Adams reported.

So how common are church shootings? Well! Lets look at some of the more infamous ones in recent history.

A total of seven people were killed when a 47-year-old Texas man opened fire during a prayer service for teen-agers at the Wedgewood Baptist Church in Fort Worth, Texas.

The gunman, identified as Larry Gene Ashbrook of Fort Worth, shouted obscenities as he emptied three ammunition magazines from a nine-millimeter, semi-automatic handgun at the gathered congregation.

Ashbrook, who authorities described as chronically unemployed and "very troubled," had six full magazines of ammunition left when he took his own life in a back pew at the church.

According to police, Ashbrook also rolled a pipe bomb down one of the church's aisles. They said the bomb exploded, but caused little damage. Nearly 150 teenagers were attending the service. Of the seven people killed, three teenagers and three adults died at the church, according to police. Another teen died later at a nearby hospital. Seven others, ranging in age from 12 to 41, were injured in the shooting. Police searched Ashbrook's house in a Fort Worth suburb. What they found was a house in a state of disarray, with holes punched in the walls and furniture upended. Torn photographs and boxes of ammunition littered the floor. "This has the appearance of being a very troubled man who for whatever reason in his own mind sought to quiet whatever demons were bothering him." FBI agent Bob Garrity told reporters at the scene.

February 14, 2010 – Richmond, California – Three hooded men walk into Gethsemane Church of God in Christ and opened fire and then fled the scene, as the singing of the choir was replaced by frightened screams. The two victims, a 14-year-old boy and a 19-year-old man, were hospitalized.

March 8, 2009 – Maryville, Illinois – Suspect Terry Joe Sedlacek, 27, of Troy, walks into the First Baptist Church and shoots pastor Fred Winters dead, point blank. The death toll would have been much higher if his gun had not jammed. Several church members are injured by a knife in the struggle to capture the attacker. The suspect also had stabbed himself, but survived. On March 29, 2013 he was deemed unfit to plead by the circuit court.

July 27, 2008 – Knoxville, Tennessee – A gunman opens fire in a church during a youth performance, killing two people and injuring seven.

Dec. 9, 2007 – Colorado – Three people are killed and five wounded in two shooting rampages, one at a missionary school in suburban Denver and one at a church in Colorado Springs. The gunman in the second incident is killed by a guard.

May 20, 2007 – Moscow, Idaho – A standoff between police and a suspect in the shootings of three people in a Presbyterian Church ended with three dead, including one police officer.

Aug. 12, 2007 – Neosho, Missouri – First Congregational Church – 3 killed – Eiken Elam Saimon shot and killed the pastor and two deacons and wounded five others.

May 21, 2006 – Baton Rouge, Louisiana – The Ministry of Jesus Christ Church – 4 killed – The four at the church who were shot were members of Erica Bell's family; she was abducted and murdered elsewhere; Bell's mother, church pastor Claudia Brown, was seriously wounded – Anthony Bell, 25, was the shooter.

Feb. 26, 2006 – Detroit, Michigan – Zion Hope Missionary Baptist Church – 2 killed + shooter – Kevin L. Collins, who reportedly went to the church looking for his girlfriend, later killed himself.

April 9, 2005 – College Park, Georgia – A 27-year-old airman died after being shot at a church, where he had once worked as a security guard.

March 12, 2005 – Brookfield, Wisconsin – Living Church of God – 7 killed + shooter – Terry Ratzmann opened fire on the congregation, killing seven and wounding four before taking his own life.

July 30, 2005 – College Park, Georgia – World Changers Church International – shooter killed – Air Force Staff Sgt. John Givens was shot five times by a police officer after charging the officer, following violent behavior.

Dec. 17, 2004, Garden Grove, Calif.: A veteran musician at the Crystal Cathedral shoots himself to death after a nine-hour standoff.

Oct. 5, 2003 – Atlanta, Georgia – Turner Monumental AME Church – 2 killed + shooter – Shelia Wilson walked into the church while preparations are being made for service and shot the pastor, her mother and then herself.

June 10, 2002 – Conception, Missouri Benedictine monastery – 2 killed + shooter – Lloyd Robert Jeffress shot four monks in the monastery killing two and wounding two, before killing himself.

March 12, 2002 – Lynbrook, New York – Our Lady of Peace Catholic Church – 2 killed – Peter Troy, a former mental patient, opens fire during Mass, killing the priest and a parishioner. He later receives a life sentence.

May 18, 2001 – Hopkinsville, Kentucky – Greater Oak Missionary Baptist Church – 2 killed - Frederick Radford stood up in the middle of a revival service and began shooting at his estranged wife, Nicole Radford, killing her and a woman trying to help her.

Sept. 15, 1999 – Fort Worth, Texas – Wedgewood Baptist Church – 7 killed + shooter – Larry Gene Ashbrook shot dead seven people and injured a further seven at a concert by Christian rock group Forty Days in Fort Worth, Texas before killing himself.

April 15, 1999 – Salt Lake City, Utah – LDS Church Family History Library – 2 killed + shooter – Sergei Babarin, 70, with a history of mental illness, entered the library, killed two people and wounded four others before he was gunned down by police.

Not all church shootings are carried out in Christian churches. The gun free zone is a rich target area for any mentally disturbed gunman looking to prove a point.

On August 5, 2012, Wade Michael Page a right wing white supremacist fatally shot six people and wounded four others in at a Sikh Temple in Oak Creek Wisconsin. The members of the Church were preparing a meal when Page entered carrying a handgun and opened fire. On leaving the unprotected church, Page encountered an armed responding police officer, Lt. Brian Murphy. The two exchanged gunfire.

The officer was hit 15 times but survived. Page was hit in the stomach and fell wounded to the ground where he killed himself with a bullet to the head before he could be arrested.

The gun free zones are of course always going to be a draw for the criminal wanting to rack up a high body count.

Should we therefore put armed guards in all our places of worship? Such places well outnumber the schools, so the idea is hardly practicable on cost alone. Add the fact that many deeply devout religious worshipers look upon firearms as instruments of violence which should have no place in the house of god.

I completely understand that point of view, but I consider myself to be both a Christian and a realist. Evil can be found everywhere, Allowing certified Concealed carry holders to carry their guns at services would not, in my opinion compromise anyone's faith.

On Saturday July 27th 2009 a Louisville Pastor, Ken Pagano from my home state of Kentucky held a service celebrating the second amendment, encouraging his congregation to bring their guns to the service. Over 200 took him up on the offer. Pastor Pagano generated a good deal of controversy, mostly from the left anti gun community.

But the message was clear enough to any would be killers who were considering a massacre in his church.

Chapter 9

The Madness of the Gun Free Military Base

*"Smooth runs the water where the brook is deep,
And in his simple show he harbors treason."*

*William Shakespeare
(King Henry the Sixth, Part II)*

Just outside the town of Killeen in bell county Texas is the most populous US military base in the world. It was named after Confederate General John Bell Hood, of the famed Texas Brigade, Fort Hood. Today the base is home to 65,000 soldiers and family members. It is at the forefront of the world war on terror with the following units being based there. Headquarters III Corps; First Army Division West; the 1st Cavalry Division; 13th Sustainment Command (formerly 13th Corps Support Command); the 89th Military police Brigade; 504th Battlefield Surveillance Brigade; 21st Cavalry Brigade (Air Combat); 4th Combat Aviation Brigade; and the 31st Air Defense Artillery Brigade.

Fort Hood also includes Carl R. Darnall Army Medical Center and the Medical And Dental Activities as tenant units. It was in that center that Army Psychiatrist Major Nidal Malik Hasan worked.

Hassan was born in Arlington Virginia His parents were both Palestinians who immigrated to the U.S. from Al-Bireh in the West Bank, reared as a Muslim together with his two younger brothers, he attended Wakefield High School in Arlington for his freshman year. After his family moved to Roanoke in 1985, he attended William Fleming High School in Roanoke. Virginia. He graduated from high school in 1988. After graduating, Hassan and his brothers helped their parents run the family's restaurant in Roanoke. Their father died in 1998 and their mother in 2001. As adults, one brother continued to live in Virginia, and the other moved to Jerusalem.

Hasan took a different path and joined the United States Army immediately after high school. He served for eight years as an enlisted soldier, while at the same time attending college. He graduated from Virginia Tech in 1995 with a bachelor's degree in biochemistry.

Hasan gained admission through a selective process for medical school at the USUHS, (Uniformed Services University of the Health Sciences). After earning his medical degree in 2003, Hasan went on to complete his internship and residency in psychiatry at the Walter Reed Army Medical Center in Washington. While an intern at Walter Reed, he received counseling and extra supervision. By taking this route Hasan was enrolled in the officer corp., a path that would see him to eventually being tasked with helping US servicemen suffering the mental stress of being in combat.

Hasan studied for a Master's in Public Health at USUHS with a two-year fellowship in Disaster and Preventive Psychiatry at the Center for Traumatic Stress at USUHS, which he completed in 2009. In May 2009, Hasan was promoted from Captain to Major before being transferred to Fort Hood in July 2009, however his religious beliefs were beginning to conflict with his military duties. He received a poor performance evaluation. Part of the reason was that he had made a presentation titled "The Koranic World View As It Relates to Muslims in the U.S. Military" during his senior year of residency at Walter Reed, which was not well received by some attendees.

In it he suggested that the Department of Defense *"should allow Muslims* [sic] *Soldiers the option of being released as "Conscientious objectors" to increase troop morale and decrease adverse events."* On a previous slide he explained that "adverse events" could be refusal to deploy, espionage or killing of fellow soldiers (as had occurred in Vietnam among other soldiers). Retired Colonel Terry Lee, who had worked with Hasan, later recalled that the fatal shooting of two recruiters in Little Rock, Arkansas on June 1st 2009, had greatly affected Hasan. The suspect in that shooting Abdulhakim Mujahid Muhammad later claimed to be an Al Qaeda terrorist. He was charged with murder. In an interview with Fox News Col. Lee stated that Hasan made "outlandish" statements against the American military presence in Iraq and Afghanistan, that "the Muslims should stand up and fight against the aggressor", referring to the US. While Hasan expressed hope that President Obama would withdraw troops. After 2004 he became more agitated, and frequently argued with soldiers. (His tendency to conflict, with aggressiveness and paranoia, were discussed by other supervisors and department heads during this period, who were concerned about his mental stability.) Despite these observations nothing was done to evaluate the officer, and like a cancer, Islamic fundamentalism slowly began to take over his rationality.

His relatives in Palestine and the U.S., who spoke to the press after the shootings, portrayed him as a quiet, peace-loving, and deeply religious man who served his country proudly, but suffered from racial harassment. His cousin Nader Hasan disputed that Hasan had ever been "disenchanted with the military", but stressed that he dreaded war after counseling soldiers who had returned with PSD (post traumatic stress disorder). He was "mortified by the idea" of deploying after having been told on a "daily basis the horrors they saw over there." Nader also claimed that Hasan had been harassed by his fellow soldiers. He had stated that he was looking at the possibility of paying back the government, for his training, to enable him to get out of the military. He was at the end of trying everything.

Hasan's aunt also said that Hasan sought discharge because of harassment relating to his Islamic faith. An army spokesman could not confirm this and The American Muslim Armed Forces and Veterans Affairs Council said that the reported harassment was "inconsistent" with their records.
His uncle Rafiq Hamad, who lives in occupied territories in Ramallah, said Hasan was a gentle and quiet man who fainted while observing childbirth, which was why he chose psychiatry. He was deeply sensitive and mourned a pet bird for months after it died.

According to the uncle, "after he lost his parents he tried to replace their love by reading a lot of books, including the Quran." Also near Ramallah, Cousin Mohammed Hasan said, "Because he's a Muslim he didn't want to go to Afghanistan or Iraq, and he didn't want to expose himself to violence and death." Mohammed stated his cousin was a "pleasant young man" who was happy to have graduated and to be joining the army after his uncle and cousins had also served. They never talked about politics, but Hasan had complained, "He was being treated like a Muslim, like an Arab, rather than an American, he was being discriminated against."

Hasan was investigated by the FBI after intelligence agencies intercepted at least 18 e-mails between him and radical terrorist Anwar al-Awlaki between December 2008 and June 2009. Even before the contents of the e-mails were revealed, terrorism expert Jarret Brachman said that Hasan's contacts with al-Awlaki should have raised "huge red flags." According to Brachman, al-Awlaki is a major influence on radical English-speaking jihadis internationally.

In one of the e-mails, Hasan wrote al-Awlaki: "I can't wait to join you" in the afterlife. Hasan also asked al-Awlaki when *jihad* is appropriate, and whether it is permissible if innocents are killed in a suicide attack.

In the months before the shooting, Hasan increased his contacts with al-Awlaki to discuss how to transfer funds abroad without coming to the attention of law authorities.

A DC-based Joint Terrorism Task Force operating under the FBI was notified of the e-mails. Its Defense Criminal Investigative Service personnel reviewed the material. Army employees were informed of the e-mails, but did not perceive any terrorist threat in Hasan's questions. Instead, they viewed them as general questions about spiritual guidance with regard to conflicts between Islam and military service, and judged them to be consistent with his legitimate mental health research about Muslims in the armed services. The assessment was that the material did not call for a larger investigation.

Following the shootings, Former Under Secretary of Homeland Security for Intelligence and Analysis, Charles Allen said this,
"I find it difficult to understand why an Army major would be in repeated contact with an Islamic extremist like Anwar al-Awlaki, who preaches a hateful ideology directed at inciting violence against the United States and the West... It is hard to see how repeated contact would in any legitimate way further his research as a psychiatrist."

Thirty nine (39) year old Hasan was a Muslim and as such was considered to be a prime example of how the US Army had integrated all religious groups into its ranks. But as we have seen, Hasan was not as patriotic as he seemed. He had secretly been corresponding by email with a radical Islamic Cleric based in Yemen Anwar al-Awlaki, an Al Queda commander, who was implicated in the attempted bombing of Northwest Airlines flight 253.

On July 31st 2009 Hasan visited the Guns Galore store in Killeen, TX and purchased a 9mm pistol. Army Specialist William Gilbert, a regular customer who was at the store that day when Hasan entered the store and asked for "the most technologically advanced weapon on the market and the one with the highest standard magazine capacity." Hasan was allegedly asked how he intended to use the weapon, but said that he wanted the most advanced handgun with the largest magazine capacity. The three people with Hasan Gilbert, the store manager, and a store employee all recommended the FN Five-seven pistol. As Gilbert personally owned one of the pistols, was happy to spend an hour describing its operation to the Army Officer.

Hasan left the store after saying he needed to research the weapon. He returned the following day and purchased the gun.

Following the purchase he continued to visit the store on a weekly basis to buy extra magazines, along with hundreds of rounds of 5.zX28mm, SS192 and SS197SR ammunition.

In the weeks that followed, Hasan visited an outdoor shooting range in Florence, where he allegedly became adept at hitting silhouette targets at distances of up to 100 yards. Having obtained and practiced with the weapon the renegade major was ready to take Al Queda's war to the heart of the US Military. He was on very safe ground, as he knew that like the schools and many public arenas, Ford Hood was a government mandated Gun Free Zone. Incredibly American troops were not allowed to carry guns on the base. They had been disarmed by a 1993 law passed by Democrat President William Clinton, which imposed a total ban on service men and women carrying personal firearms on the base, and also made it virtually impossible for base commanders to issue firearms for protection of the troops. Only the Military Police were permitted to carry side arms but their numbers on the base were woefully inadequate to offer any real protection.

On November 5th 2009 at approximately 1:34 pm local time, Hasan entered his workplace, the Soldier Readiness Processing Center, where service personnel receive routine medical treatment immediately prior to and on return from deployment. His presence was barely noticed, as he was a frequent visitor. What was not known was that he was armed with the FN five seven pistol, which he had fitted with two LaserMax Laser sights one red, and one green.

According to eyewitnesses, Hasan had taken a seat at an empty table and bowed his head for several seconds apparently in prayer when he suddenly stood up, and shouted "Allahu Akbar! (God is Great in Arabic) and opened fire. Witnesses said Hasan initially "sprayed bullets at soldiers in a fanlike motion" before taking aim at individual soldiers. Eyewitness Sgt. Michael Davis said: *"The rate of fire was pretty much constant shooting. When I initially heard it, it sounded like an M16."*

Army reserve Captain John Gaffaney tried to stop the mad Hasan by charging him, but was mortally wounded before reaching him. Civilian physician assistant Michael Cahill also tried to charge Hasan with a chair, but he too was shot and killed.

Army reserve Specialist Logan Burnett tried to stop Hasan by throwing a folding table at him, but he was shot in the left hip, he collapsed but managed to crawl into a nearby cubicle. Chairs and bare hands were the only weapons at the soldiers' disposal. The courage of the US Military has never been in doubt. The sanity of its political leaders, well that's a different matter.

According to testimony from witnesses, Hasan targeted soldiers in uniform, ignoring the civilians present. As stated these soldiers were not allowed to carry personal firearms on the base due to Clinton's law. At one point, Hasan reportedly approached a group of five civilians hiding under a desk. He looked at them, swept the dot of his pistol's laser sight over one of the men's faces, and turned away without firing. The shooting had raised the alarm and although the military had been disarmed there were civilian police on the base, one of these was Sergeant Kimberly Munley, who rushed to the scene in her patrol car. The first officer to arrive, she encountered Hasan in the area outside the Soldier Readiness Processing Center. Hasan immediately fired at her. Munley returned fire, exchanging shots with him using her 9mm M9 pistol. The exchange ended when Munley's hand was hit by shrapnel, when one of Hasan's bullets struck a nearby rain gutter, and then two more bullets struck Munley herself. The first bullet hit her thigh and the second her knee.

As she began to fall from the first bullet, the second bullet struck her femur, shattering it and knocking her to the ground. Her gun falling clear, Hasan walked up to Munley and kicked the pistol out of reach.

As the shooting continued outside, nurses and medics entered the building, fearing Hasan's return they secured the doors with a belt and rushed to help the wounded. According to the responding nurses, there was so much blood covering the floor inside the building that they were unable to maintain balance and had difficulty reaching the many wounded to help them. In the area outside the building, Hasan continued to shoot at fleeing soldiers, and civilian police.

A second civilian police officer, Sergeant Mark Todd arrived and shouted at Hasan to surrender. Hasan turned and fired twice at him. Hasan missed but Todd didn't, 5 rounds struck the Major knocking him down. Todd ran over kicked the pistol out of his hand and put handcuffs on him as the wounded man fell unconscious.

An investigation later revealed that 146 spent shell casings were recovered inside the building and another 68 casings were collected outside, making a total a total of 214 rounds fired by the attacker and responding civilian police officers.

A medic who later treated Hasan said his pockets were full of loaded pistol magazines. When the shooting ended, he was still carrying 177 rounds of unfired ammunition in his pockets, contained in both 20- and 30-round magazines. The incident had only lasted about 10 minutes but had resulted in 13 deaths, 12 soldiers and one civilian; 11 died at the scene, and two died later in a hospital; and 30 people wounded.

The two faces of Major Nidal Hasan
before and after the shootings.

Despite the overwhelming evidence that this was an al Queda inspired attack, the President, Barak Obama refused to acknowledge this and it was officially logged as a work related violence incident. This of course meant none of the injuries were classed as combat related, and no awards could be considered and most of all, the President hoped that no one would notice that Fort Hood was a gun free zone.

On November 5, 2010, one year later, 52 individuals did received awards for their actions in the shooting. The Soldiers Medal was awarded to 10 soldiers, including Captain John Gaffaney, who died trying to charge the shooter. The Secretary of the Army Award for Valor was awarded to police officers Kimberly Munley and Mark Todd for the roles they played in stopping the shooter.

On May 23, 2011, the Army Award for Valor was posthumously awarded to the civilian physician assistant Michael Cahill, who died trying to charge the shooter with a chair. In May 2012, US Senator Joe Lieberman and Representative Peter T. King proposed legislation that would make the victims of the shooting eligible for the Purple Heart. This was denied as the event had already been classed as work violence so the soldiers injuries could not be considered combat related.

Soon after the attack, Al Queda commander Anwar al-Awlaki posted praise for Hasan for the shooting on his website.

He wrote,
"Nidal Hasan is a hero, the fact that fighting against the U.S. army is an Islamic duty today cannot be disputed. Nidal has killed soldiers who were about to be deployed to Iraq and Afghanistan in order to kill Muslims."[In March 2010, Al-Awlaki alleged that the Obama administration tried to portray Hasan's actions as an individual act of violence from an estranged individual, and that it was trying to suppress information for the American public. "

Obviously Awlaki was fully aware that the attack was linked to the war on Terror. His mention of troop deployment proves that. Also, Hasan's desire to target only soldiers and Hasan's shout of "Allahu Akbar!" (A typical battle cry of terrorists before an assault) are pretty convincing evidence that Hasan at least felt he was fighting for Islam. On September 10, 2010, the Bipartisan policy Centre released the report *'Assessing the Terrorist Threat',* which concluded that "in 2009 at least 43 American citizens or residents aligned with Sunni militant groups or their ideology were charged or convicted of terrorism crimes in the U.S. or elsewhere, the highest number in any year since 9/11."

They listed the Fort Hood shooting and the 2009 shooting at Little Rock Recruiting Office as two successful terrorist attacks, but neither case has been prosecuted as such. On November 5, 2012, 3 years after the attack, 148 plaintiffs, including victims and families of victims, filed a wrongful death against the United States Government, Hasan, and the estate of Anwar al-Awlaki. Their lawsuit alleges there were due process violations, intentional misrepresentation, assault and battery, gross negligence, and civil conspiracy. Since his detention Hasan has grown a beard, refusing to shave it off, and maintaining it is against his religion to do so. An impediment he did not seem to have prior to the assault. This and other delaying tactics have prevented the trial from going ahead. At the time of this writing March 2013, Hasan is still awaiting trial.

Chapter 10

The Mindset of the Armed Criminal

All the multiple-victim public shootings in Western Europe have occurred in places where civilians are not permitted to carry guns. The same is true in the United States: All the public shootings in which more than three people have been killed have occurred in places where civilians may not legally bring guns.

John R Lott, National Review on line

A fundamental flaw in the idea that creating gun free zones is the misunderstanding of the criminal who carry's the gun. Firstly, it should be understood that a criminal is a lawbreaker, which means a person who blatantly breaks the law. From the criminals point of view carrying a firearm gives him an edge. It will enable him to compel his victims to do his will. The greatest fear he (or she) faces is that his victim may also be armed. Therefore their course is obvious. Go to an area where you can be fairly sure there will be no armed opposition.

Secondly criminals live outside the boundaries that most of us live by. They have little regard for the rule of law.

They are already breaking the law and therefore see no problem in breaking the law of the Gun Free Zone, should it suit their end. A law is nothing but an agreement that civilized society comes up with that a group of people want to live by. Usually motivated by greed or resentment of authority, the criminal sees the efforts of the gun control lobby as very helpful to their lifestyle.

To make it worse, certain left wing politicians also advocate the publishing of names and addresses of concealed carry holders. They quote the Freedom of Information Act 1966 as their authority for such demands. Strange, that they support this Act but fervently oppose the US Constitution, the foundation of all US Law. When you closely examine such a proposal it becomes clear to anyone, that where most concealed carry holders would not be affected by such disclosures, the names missing from the list would be very useful to the armed criminal. Christmas of 2012 brought this into sharp focus when a New York newspaper published the names and addresses of handgun permit holders in the county. This caused an outcry and the paper was flooded with complaints.

However in my opinion, the outcry was mainly over privacy and prejudice against gun owners.

The gun owners were not really in danger, but the paper did the criminals a great service by identifying the houses that would offer armed resistance as opposed to the ones that would not. This is the sort of consequences such politically motivated stunts bring about.

Statistics show that Washington D.C. enacted a virtual ban on handguns in 1976. Between that year and 1991, Washington D.C.'s homicide rate rose 200%, while the U.S. rate rose 12%. In a Fatal Accident graph total, deaths by firearms ranks at the bottom: 1.5% but raises to 2.7% when attributed to deaths of children 14 and under. One has to worry more about car accidents, which ranked number one, than of accidental gun deaths. So what do the criminals feel about the likelihood of their victims being able to defend themselves? In 1993 The Department of Justice carried out a survey in an effort to find out what they thought. The survey was carried out by two professors, James D. Wright and Peter H. Rossi. Their report was published in 1986 under the title *Armed and Considered Dangerous: a survey of felons and their firearms. .)*

The academics interviewed over 1800 prison inmates in ten different states. The survey results proved bad news for the anti gun lobby.

Fifty-seven percent of those felons agreed, "Most criminals are more worried about meeting an armed victim then they are about running into the police." Fifty-six percent agreed that no one is going to mess around with a victim that he knows is armed with a gun."
Seventy-four percent agreed that "one reason burglars avoid houses when people are at home is that they fear being shot", and fifty-eight percent agreed, "a store owner who is known to keep a gun on the premises is not going to get robbed very often."

I broached this same subject with my local city Police Chief in 2011 and he confirmed that in his experience most criminals he had met in the course of his duties had held similar fears.
So moving on from that, we should examine the role of the armed citizen, the non police officer who carries a weapon concealed and how his presence affects criminal activity.

The celebrated armed defense expert Massad Ayoob reported on a conversation he had with Ron Borsch, instructor at the Southeast Area Law Enforcement Academy in Ohio, while the two met at annual conference of ILEETA, the International Law Enforcement Educators, and Trainers Association in January 2012.

Borsch's impromptu discussion revealed the fact that some 25% of mass murder shooting sprees he has researched was ended by armed private citizens.

This led in turn to a discussion of the Israeli Model, in place since the Ma'alot massacre of schoolchildren decades ago, in which teachers and other school personnel were trained and discreetly armed with handguns, which has proven famously successful ever since in Israel.

Across the ten-member panel AND the dozens of police instructors attending the discussion, not a single voice was raised against that concept, and many spoke enthusiastically in favor of it. However the countless cases of armed citizens defending themselves and saving lives are rarely reported in the mainstream media. A local station may make brief comment, but usually tries to avoid any suggestion that the homeowner acted correctly. It is left to groups like The NRA and Gun owners of America to fill the void and try and redress the balance. The monthly NRA magazines carry details of personal defense incidents but they are restricted to NRA membership and therefore, the NRA is preaching to the converted. Could armed citizens have prevented some of the more infamous killings in the USA, who can say, but the implementation of gun free zones ensured they would never get the chance.

Chapter 11

New York City's Defiance of the Second Amendment

"They've promised that dreams can come true - but forgot to mention that nightmares are dreams, too."

Oscar Wilde

The city of New York comes under particular criticism from the pro gun lobby, as its city ordinances and legislators seem to continually defy the second amendment and therefore the US Constitution. At the forefront of this criticism is its Mayor Michael Bloomberg.
Bloomberg is a billionaire whose wealth was put at $19.5 billion in 2011. A former life long Democrat, Bloomberg left that party and joined the Republican Party in 2001. This appears to have been purely a political move. As a Republican he was able to run for mayor riding the tide of patriotism sweeping the country in the aftermath of 911, when the nation was rallying around the Republican President George W. Bush and its outgoing Mayor Rudi Giuliani.

Having won the election primarily by spending $73 million of his own money, Bloomberg distanced himself from his republican colleagues and finally left the party in 2007 to fight the 2008 election as an independent. Having won the election he immediately campaigned to have the New York term limits changed to allow him to keep fighting elections and retain his grip on power, assisted by a massive personal fortune his critics understandably say he simply bought the mayor-ship.

His stances on giving permanent residency to illegal immigrants, and support for a mosque adjacent to the ground zero site did not exactly endear him to the residents of NYC or the Republican Party, but it was his heavy anti- gun policy that really put him in the crosshairs of the NRA.

Bloomberg formed the group "Mayors Against Illegal Guns," (MAIG), an eye-catching title that was designed to appeal to the law-abiding community, but in reality was a pressure group for stricter gun control.

There are 600 members of this coalition but there is far from consensus among them. Twelve of the members had resigned by 2009 after they realized the true agenda of the group.

These members are as follows,

Mayor Jared Fuhriman	Idaho Falls, Idaho
Mayor James Brainard	Carmel, Indiana
Mayor Kevin Jackson	Rio Rancho, New Mexico
Mayor Mark Begich	Anchorage, Alaska
Mayor Harry Moore	Oldham Township, New Jersey
Mayor Marlene Anielski	Walton Hills, Ohio
Mayor Mary B. Wolf	Williamsport, Pennsylvania
Mayor Patricia Shontz	Madeira Beach, Florida
Mayor Bill Haslam	Knoxville, Tennessee
Mayor Ernest B. Wiggins	Warsaw, Indiana
Mayor Dave Munson	Sioux Falls, South Dakota
Mayor Bill White	Houston, Texas

In her resignation letter, Mayor Patricia Shontz of Madeira Beach, Florida wrote, "I am withdrawing because I believe the MAIG is attempting to erode all gun ownership, not just illegal guns.

Additionally, I have learned that the MAIG may be working on issues which conflict with legal gun ownership." She added, "It appears the MAIG has misrepresented itself to the Mayors of America and its citizens. This is gun control, not crime prevention."

In his resignation letter to Bloomberg, Mayor Harry Moore stated:

"It is simply unconscionable that this coalition, under your leadership, would call for a repeal of the Shelby /Tiahrt amendment that helps to safeguard criminal investigations and the lives of law enforcement officers, witnesses and others by restricting access to firearms trace data solely to law enforcement. How anyone, least of all a public official, could be willing to sacrifice such a law enforcement lifeline in order to gain an edge in suing an industry they have political differences with is repugnant to me. The fact that your campaign against this protective language consisted of overheated rhetoric, deception and falsehoods is disturbing."

Both these mayors realized that Mayor Bloomberg's agenda has nothing to do with reducing gun crime or crime in general. It is all about reducing gun ownership to a level where it can be eliminated entirely.

Disturbing indeed, but such criticism is unlikely to have much effect. With unlimited funds available to promote his agenda the nefarious New York Mayor will no doubt continue his campaign. Groups like the NRA will be hard pressed to counter such expenditure.

The resignations of Kevin Jackson and Jared Fuhriman left the state of Idaho completely unrepresented in the organization, and Alaska with just one representative mayor. Since Mayor Rocky Anderson of Salt Lake City left office, it has also left Utah unrepresented. Mayor Kathy Taylor of Tulsa, Oklahoma has announced that she will not seek re-election, and as of September 2009, her name has been removed from the coalition's roster. This also leaves Oklahoma unrepresented. According to the U.S. Conference of Mayors there are 1,201 cities in the US with a population of 30,000 or more that are headed by mayors.

Several of the mayors in the Mayors Against Illegal Guns coalition represent even smaller towns and cities--particularly in New Jersey and Pennsylvania, which are disproportionately represented.
While MAIG is an arm of NYC's anti gun policies it is by no means the only one.

The city of New York has its own codes in addition to the Second Amendment. Article 2, Section 4 of the New York Civil Rights Law provides; "A well regulated militia being necessary to the security of a free state, the right of the people to keep and bear arms cannot be infringed." On the face of it no restrictions on gun possession can be permitted Right?

Wrong, at least in the eyes of Mayor Bloomberg. In NYC it is illegal to possess any rifle, pistol, or shotgun without a permit. The application fee for a permit is $140.00. You must also pay a fingerprint fee of $94.25.

A license is needed to possess a handgun in one's home or place of business. Application is made to the licensing officer of the city or county where the applicant resides, is principally employed, or where his principal place of business as a merchant or storekeeper is located.

An alien may obtain a pistol license if he or she meets these requirements.
The determination whether to grant the license is completely within the discretion of the licensing officer. However, the licensing officer must state specifically and concisely in writing the reasons for a denial. A denial can only be overturned in court if the denial is shown to be arbitrary and capricious.

A license may be granted to an applicant who is of good moral character, who is over 21 years of age, who has not been convicted of a serious offense, who states if and when he has ever been treated for mental illness, who is not subject to a protective court order and to whom no good cause exists for the denial of the license.

The age requirement shall not apply to persons honorably discharged from the military. (Persons between age 18 and 21 may possess a handgun at an indoor or outdoor pistol range located in or on premises owned or occupied by a duly incorporated organization organized for conservation purposes or to foster proficiency in small arms. A person between the ages of 18 and 21 may also possess a handgun at a target pistol shooting competition under the auspices of or approved by the NRA and while under immediate supervision).

An investigation will be conducted regarding all statements required in the application. This includes taking the fingerprints and physical descriptive data of the applicant.
One copy of the fingerprints will be forwarded to the FBI for a search of the applicant's criminal records. The failure or refusal of the FBI to make the fingerprint check shall not constitute the sole basis for refusal to issue a permit.

The licensing officer may, in his discretion, add restrictions to the license, limiting the places where the handgun may be kept or carried. No demonstration of need to possess is required to obtain an "on premises only," license valid for one's home or place of business. A demonstration of need must be shown, however, for a license not restricted to one of those locations.

An "on premises only" license authorizes the possession of a handgun only at the location written on the license. It does not authorize the holder to take such handgun to any other place. (It should be noted further that an "on premises only" license technically does not authorize the holder even to transport the handgun from its place of purchase to the location stated on the license.)

Applications for licenses must be acted upon within 6 months after presentment. If there is a delay, there must be written notice to the applicant stating the reasons. Such delay may be excused for good cause only.

If issued, a license is valid until revoked, except in New York City where a license shall expire not more than 3 years after the date of issuance, and in Nassau, Suffolk, and Westchester Counties where a license shall expire not more than 5 years after the date of issuance. The ordinance for gun possession is certainly restrictive and in my opinion clearly an infringement of the right of the people to keep and bear arms. With an ever-growing membership, I expect the NRA,ILA to challenge these clear violations of the US Constitution in due course.

The case of Mark Meckler, Tea Party Patriot's co-founder; is a good illustration of the way NYC laws effectively work against the US Constitution.

In 2011 Meckler was travelling through La Guardia Airport when he was arrested by New York City police. The charge, C Violent Felony of Possession of a Firearm with Intent to Use; so what was it that Mr. Meckler had actually done, (Other than stupidly assuming that NYC would operate under the same federal laws that govern other airports in the country.)

The following is a statement from Mark Meckler that I reproduced with his permission.

It shows the nightmare he endured.
On December 15, 2011 at approximately 5:15 a.m., I was at LaGuardia International airport preparing to check in for a flight out of the city. During a routine check-in, I requested a firearms declaration form from the ticket agent. It was my intent to declare and check my unloaded firearm. I purchased this firearm legally, and I have a valid concealed carry permit for it issued in California. The unloaded gun was locked inside a TSA-approved travel case, and the case was locked inside my checked luggage. I carry the firearm for my personal safety, having received numerous threats due to my role in the Tea Party Patriots. I have checked this firearm at airports dozens of times before, all across the country.

As I traveled through LaGuardia that morning, I passed TSA signs telling me I had the right to check this unloaded firearm in my luggage, and that I am required by law to declare the firearm to the ticketing agent. This is exactly what I did. The ticketing agent provided me with the declaration form, and I signed it and returned it to her. She advised me that she would need to call Port Authority police to inspect. This is not unusual when traveling with a firearm. Procedures vary from airport to airport, from airline to airline, and even from day to day, and as a law-abiding citizen, I have always been happy to cooperate.

Unfortunately, that day, I didn't realize that I was about to cross paths with New York City's anti-Second Amendment stance. Upon showing my case and the weapon to the officer who arrived on the scene, and after a few brief questions, she advised me that she was placing me under arrest for violating New York City's firearms laws.

To say that I was stunned would be an understatement. I am from a law enforcement family. My mother is a retired correctional officer, and I have spent my life around folks from the law enforcement community. I have always considered myself a law-abiding citizen. I have never been arrested before. I have never been in police custody. I can never say those things again.

On December 15th, 2011, I was arrested, handcuffed at the ticket counter, and taken to a waiting squad car for transport to the Port Authority Police station at LaGuardia.
I was subsequently transferred, in handcuffs, to the Queens Central booking facility in New York City. I was charged with felony possession of a firearm with intent to do harm. I spent the day in Queens...in jail.
It was a nightmare that I can scarcely describe to you. Until you have felt the handcuffs on your wrists, and until you have heard that cell door close behind you, it is impossible to understand what it means to actually lose *your liberty.*

And since that day, my liberty has been at stake, and because of that threat, based upon the advice of counsel; I've been unable to speak publicly about this case. Today the silence ends.
I am pleased to announce that the criminal case against me has been dropped. Although I was originally charged with a violent felony, the case against me was resolved with a plea to "disorderly conduct." Disorderly Conduct is not a felony or a misdemeanor, or even a crime. The facts underlying my plea are that I declared a legally purchased, properly licensed and unloaded firearm at an airport counter.

Apparently, much to my surprise, in New York City, it is considered "disorderly conduct" to exercise your constitutionally guaranteed, Second Amendment rights.

Strangely, now that the case against me is over, the authorities refuse to return my firearm. There is no law that allows them to confiscate a weapon in this manner. They simply say "no" when you ask for your weapon back. This is apparently their "policy." It is done regularly in New York. This is government robbery. Not only is New York City anti-Second Amendment rights, but they are depriving citizens of their legally owned property. My lawyer has advised me that I can attempt to pursue the return of my firearm but that to do so would cost me more than the firearm is worth. I am not alone in facing this tyranny.

It has happened to hundreds of people in the New York metro area. My lawyer, Brian Stapleton has handled over 400 of these cases himself, so he is an expert on the subject.

While the end of this case is the end of a horrible nightmare for my family and I, it is not the end of this fight. It is just the beginning. Since the original incident, I have received more emails, phone calls, texts and tweets of support than you can imagine. To those people, I want to say heartfelt thanks on behalf of my entire family. We have come to know that we are not alone in this particular fight. Apparently, this happens to hundreds of people per year in New York City.

And New York City is not alone in its attack on our rights. This sort of Constitutional abuse, Second Amendment and otherwise, is taking place all over the nation. And we as citizens must stand against it. We must protect our rights, or we will lose them.

Unfortunately the case of Mark Meckler was not the only one to highlight the absurdity of Bloomberg's laws. Take the case of 39 year old Tennessee tourist Merideth Graves, a concealed carry permit holder, who on December 22nd 2011 was in NYC for a job interview and decided to visit the 9/11 memorial. On arrival she noticed a no guns allowed sign at the entrance and as she was carrying a gun she enquired where she could check it in with the police.
She was directed to a police officer, who immediately arrested her for breaching the city's gun laws. Of course Ms Graves had no criminal intent. The fact that she had approached the police herself proved that, but the law of course was not designed to keep lawbreakers from carrying guns in NYC. Bloomberg's law was simply imposed to eliminate gun possession by its residents. A fact confirmed when he refused to allow the National Guard to assist in rescue operations in NYC after hurricane sandy struck the city in November 2012. He stating
" The NYPD are the only people we want on the street with guns."

147

Such stupidity is almost beyond belief, but is part of life for the suffering residents of New York City. By the end of January 2013, thousands of residents of New York were still without power or heat. But following Sandy Hook, the mayor spent little time in NYC he was travelling out of State pushing the gun control agenda with his pressure group and President Barak Obama.
While Mayor Bloomberg was not the only Democrat to use tragedy to advance his own gun agenda, he was the most prominent.

On January 15th 2013 The States Governor Andrew Cuomo, rushed through a new set of gun laws, without waiting for President Obama's proposals, due out the following day.
The new laws include a statewide gun registry and a uniform licensing standard, altering the current system in which each county or municipality sets its own standard. Residents are now restricted to purchasing ammunition magazines that carry seven rounds, rather than 10. Because of this zealots haste to pass the law without discussion or debate, he forgot to include any exemptions to his law, thus making most police officers and all secret service agents' criminals overnight, as their Glocks and Berettas held 10 to 15 rounds. Not to mention the ARs held in their inventory. A quick amendment was passed through, but the whole incident castes serious doubt on the competency of a man to govern a major US State.

Although Cuomo's measures did include new laws on mental health monitoring and a law banning the publication of the names and addresses of gun owners (Better late than never), let us make no mistake. The new laws created the toughest gun control measures in the USA. As we have seen, the laws will have ZERO effect on the criminal. They will of course place homeowners trying to defend themselves at a distinct disadvantage. So long as the home invader is armed with a small handgun, it may be a fair fight. But most will ensure they have all the firepower they need to overcome a homeowner. Most likely anyone trying to resist will be facing an AK47 or AR15, wielded by a criminal who didn't get Cuomo's memo.

The Gun Free Killing Zones of America

Chapter 12

California the Tarnished
Golden State

"I may not agree with you, but I will defend to the death your right to make an ass of yourself."

Oscar Wilde.

The most populous state in the USA, California is a bit of an enigma. The State has become a byword for fringe and Left Wing Politics. Everything from Gay Marriage, to legalizing drugs and setting up sanctuary cities to offering support to illegal immigrants, has made California a target for Republican and right wing groups.
It is currently (2012) Democratically controlled with a Democrat Governor, Lt Governor, 2 Democrat Senators, 34 democrat and 19 Republican house US members.

Although gun rights are more or less intact, severe restrictions have been placed on the States gun owners by the States legislators. The California anti gun charge is led by its two Democratic senators Diane Feinstein and Barbara Boxer.

These two ladies have kept up a tirade of ill thought out policies that have contributed to this former great states downfall.

Let us have a look at what weapons allowed under "Bureau of Alcohol, Tobacco, Firearms," (BATF) regulations but banned under California State Law. Short-barreled rifles, cane guns, wallet guns, undetectable firearms, and firearms not immediately recognizable as a firearm, are all illegal. Camouflaging firearms containers, and all ammunition containing or consisting of a flechette dart, explosive bullets, ballistic knives, multi-burst trigger activators, Nunchakus, metal knuckles, belt buckle knives, leaded canes, zip guns, shuriken, unconventional pistols, lipstick case knives, cane swords, shobi-zue, air gauge knives, writing pen knives, metal practice and even replica hand grenades are prohibited. Other items also banned are, weapons commonly known as blackjacks, slingshots, Billy-clubs, sand clubs, saps or sandbags. This section also prohibits carrying concealed upon the person any dirk or dagger. Even though the BATF may have sent out a letter stating that an item is not deemed to be a firearm or destructive device under federal law, the California Penal code contains multiple definitions of destructive devices. The mere possession of which in California may subject you to felony prosecution.

For example, 37 mm launchers are regularly offered for mail order sale in publications like "The Shotgun News." The BATF sent out a letter stating that these launchers are considered both firearms and destructive devices only when they are possessed along with "anti-personnel ammunition" such as riot control cartridges containing wood pellets, rubber pellets or balls, or beanbags. However, the same BATF direction also states that these launchers are neither firearms nor destructive devices (and therefore not subject to federal control) when possessed only with pyrotechnic (e.g. "bird bombs" or "star burst distress flares") or tear gas cartridges. The potential "legal trap" is that there have been prosecutions in California for possession of these 37 mm launchers that were possessed only with pyrotechnic cartridges. The reason is aggressive District Attorneys have used the broadly worded California definitions of destructive devices and fireworks to prosecute California any gun owner in possession who assumed these items were legal because they were able to acquire them from commercial sources. This is a common mistake and also applies to Armor Piercing ammunition, often advertised on line on mail order sites such as Gunbroker.com.

Even certain guns classified as conventional firearms under federal law, are declared unlawful in California.

For example, the popular Thompson Contender single shot pistol, when equipped or possessed with a combination .45 Colt/.410 shotgun barrel or just the barrel itself, is illegal in California as it is somewhat ludicrously considered a short-barreled shotgun. The BATF does not consider it a sawed-off shotgun because the barrel is rifled rather than smooth bore. Shotguns are defined as smooth bore weapons.

Tracer ammunition (Other than that for use in shotguns) is illegal in California, as it is included in the definition of a destructive device; possession of even a single round of World War II 30-06 tracer ammunition can subject you to felony prosecution.

Unwitting California gun owners have even been arrested and prosecuted for possession of exploding targets of the type popularized in TV shows like Top Shot. This is because, The California Health and Safety Code Section contains a broad definition of fireworks that include devices that produce, by combustion, an audio or visual effect for entertainment. Assault weapons, these have their own classification under the Unique anti gun laws of California. Broadly they are defined as follows,

In the Roberti-Roos "Assault Weapons Control Act" of 1989 (AWCA) the California Legislature defined Assault Weapons by listing specific makes and models. Those named firearms remain Assault Weapons and cannot be lawfully imported into California. Far more firearms were classified as Assault Weapons by certain generic characteristics effective January 1, 2000. To determine if a firearm which you may intend to bring into the state you will need to pay particular attention to the characteristics of your firearm and check it against the statutory language of the Law. California Penal Code section 12276.1 An Assault weapon, is further defined under The California Penal Code (Section 12276.1) as -
1. Any semiautomatic center fire rifle that has the capacity to accept a detachable magazine and any one of the following;
A pistol grip that protrudes conspicuously beneath the action of the weapon,
A thumbhole stock,
A folding or telescoping stock,
A grenade launcher or flare launcher,
A flash suppressor,
A forward pistol grip.
2. A semiautomatic center fire rifle that has a fixed magazine with the capacity to accept more than 10 rounds.
3. A semiautomatic center fire rifle that has an overall length of less than 30 inches.

4. A semiautomatic pistol that has the capacity to accept a detachable magazine and and has one of the following;

A threaded barrel, capable of accepting a flash suppressor, forward handgrip, or silencer.

A second handgrip.

A shroud that is attached to, or partially or completely encircles, the barrel that allows the bearer to fire the weapon without burning his or her hand, except a slide that encloses the barrel.

The capacity to accept a detachable magazine at some location outside the pistol grip.

5. A semiautomatic pistol with a fixed magazine that has the capacity to accept more than 10 rounds.

6. A semiautomatic shotgun that has both of the following:

A folding or telescoping stock.

A pistol grip that protrudes conspicuously beneath the action of the weapon, thumbhole stock, or vertical handgrip.

7. A semiautomatic shotgun that has the ability to accept a detachable magazine.

8. Any shotgun with a revolving cylinder.

Further, California Penal Code § 12278 specifies that any rife that can fire a .50 BMG cartridge is an Assault Weapon, and therefore such rifles are generally not importable.

With all these restrictive gun laws on the California Statute books, you would think that gun crime has been all but eliminated right! Well No not exactly. According to FBI data, California had the most gun murders in 2010, 257, which is 69 percent of all murders in 2010.

Nevertheless, California gun murders are still down by 8 percent from the previous year. Broken down by firearms murder rate per 100,000 people, the District of Columbia is number one on the list, with 16 firearms murders per 100,000 people. The District of D.C. also topped the list of firearm robberies per 100,000 people with 255.98. Yet The District of Columbia arguably has the tightest gun laws in the country. So what is happening?
Well! At the same time that violent crime rates have been falling across the USA, gun ownership has risen sharply. People worried that the Obama administration would bring in further restrictions on gun ownership.

Chapter 13

The Politicians who Stand Against the Second Amendment

Diane Feinstein

In April 2000 Sen. Dianne Feinstein, the author of the new failing Assault Weapons Ban, unveiled another gun control proposal that would require federally approved licensing of all owners of handguns and certain semi-automatic weapons. Under her plan, applicants for gun licenses would have to pay $25 and go to one of 100,000 federally licensed firearms dealers or to a state-certified office. The dealer or state-approved official would then record the gun sale and licensing with the Treasury Department. Applicants would be required to submit a thumbprint, photograph, their name, birthplace, and address, and sign a statement swearing that the information is accurate. They would also have to pass a written firearms test, akin to a driver's test, that would pose questions about the safe handling of firearms and the owners' legal responsibility.

The licenses would be renewable every five years and could be revoked.

Feinstein said her plan is intended to keep handguns and semi-automatic firearms away from criminals, people with mental disabilities, and children. This idea made her popular with the Brady group and anti gun supporters, but not the 80 million gun owners of America. It also showed a total lack of comprehension of the Second Amendment and also a fundamental ignorance of the reasons the American citizens want to retain their right to own and use guns.

The fact that criminals totally ignore gun laws and those responsible parents teach their children the safe use of firearms when hunting, and the right of self- defense. Needless to say her bill was doomed to failure when wiser and more rational minds prevailed.

Nor was her bill the only radical plans this left wing Senator supported. She also voted against private sales at gun shows and severe restrictions on their operation. Against proposal to allow Amtrak to transport passengers' firearms in securely sealed baggage cars and to hold gun manufacturers responsible for any crimes committed with their products. Although these bills all failed when they reached congress this lady has made no secret of her desire to eliminate guns from US Society, legal guns that is. None of her proposals of course had any effect on the use of illegal weapons.

However Senator Feinstein's position as a senior member of the Senate and Chairman of the House intelligence committee makes her a dangerous opponent. I do not have too many problems with this lady, as a shrewd investigator of US foreign policy and her duties in the house; however she is dangerously misguided on her attempts to undermine the Second Amendment.

In doing so she is opposing the Constitution of the United States. A document, that as a Senator she is sworn to uphold.

Senator Barbara Boxer

Senator Boxer's support for the so-called Assault Weapons ban, the support for lawsuits against gun manufacturers, for any gun violence incident using that company's products as well as her attempts to ban private gun sales at gun shows got the feisty senator an "F" rating from the NRA. Senator Boxer has been a sponsor of bills to ban compact handguns, such as those commonly carried for protection. She did this by proposing making the legality of their manufacture in the U.S. contingent upon the Bureau of Alcohol, Tobacco, Firearms, and Explosives' (BATFE) regulation permitting the same type of firearm to be imported.

It is intriguing how many different ways politicians can invent to undermine the Second Amendment. Every one of course is an infringement. So everyone fails.

Senator Charles Schumer

A Democrat from New York is another prominent Anti Second Amendment lawmaker. The sponsor of legislation to ban firearms as "assault weapons," to ban hunting, recreational, target practice and defensive ammunition as "armor piercing," and to impose a waiting period on handgun sales.

Despite this he sees no conflict with his oath to uphold the Constitution and his fanatic attempts to outlaw the second Amendment. This member of Congress is one who most seeks publicity for himself on gun control issues and is unlikely to baulk at ignoring other parts of the US Constitution that he does not agree with.

Congresswoman Jackie Speier

California's 14th Congressional District. Jackie Speier is another Democrat who is proud of her record of infringing the right of the people to keep and bear arms. On her website Ms Speier praises the anti 2nd Amendment stance of her State. We banned assault weapons in California almost 20 years ago and the world did not end.

California has a 10-day waiting period and requires background checks on all gun purchases. (So does Connecticut) You actually have to pass a safety class and have a permit to buy a handgun in California. And California's firearm homicide rate has been cut in half over the past 20 years.

As stated prior in this writing, the congresswoman omitted to say was that California still has the 2nd highest murder rate in the USA. According to FBI data, California had the most gun murders in 2010, 257, which is 69 percent of all murders in 2010.

Nevertheless, California gun murders are still down by 8 percent from the previous year. So this is the figure she pushes, in the vain hope that no one will check the facts.

Carolyn McCarthy New York

Carolyn McCarthy, Democrat, ran for Congress for one reason: gun control. For her, the issue was personal. McCarthy, a registered Republican who had worked as a nurse, began speaking out in favor of gun control after the Long Island Rail Road shooting. In 1996, her Congressman, Rep. Daniel Frisa, a Republican, announced that he planned to vote to repeal the federal Assault Weapons Ban. He was mounting his re-election campaign at the same time that McCarthy was advocating for tougher gun laws.

McCarthy challenged him for the seat, and won, changing her allegiance and becoming a Democrat. Since then, McCarthy has pushed for gun-control measures as her signature issue in Congress, including the National Instant Check System Improvement Amendments Act of 2007, which strengthened background checks by including mental-health records in the federal background-check system for gun purchasers. President Bush signed it into law almost seven months after the 2007 Virginia Tech shooting, with backing from the NRA.

That was the first major gun-control legislation Congress had passed in more than 12 years, the Brady Campaign to Prevent Gun Violence proudly said at the time, with the Assault Weapons Ban having expired in 2004, and without any significant gun laws passed since McCarthy's bill became law in 2008.

After the Newtown, Conn., elementary school shooting the New York Democratic congresswoman from Long Island has threatened to "embarrass" President Obama if he doesn't take action on gun control. Of course the muddled Congresswoman has long been a figure of fun from gun owners after such an answer she gave to a question on assault weapons. The question came in 2004 when the ban expired.

She was asked, what is a barrel shroud? (One of the components she was pushing to ban). After some blustering, the congresswoman confidently announced that she understood it was the fold out thing from the back.

In my opinion any elected official who does not have the basic knowledge of firearms, should never be in a position to legislate laws on them.

Andrew Cuomo

As governor of New York, Andrew Cuomo has consistently backed Mayor Bloomberg in his quest to outlaw guns. In March 2013 he rushed through the most ill thought out gun laws in the States history. It is widely believed that this legislation was written by the Brady group supported by Mayor Bloomberg, and at least one member of the States legislator concurred with this view.

As stated in the previous chapter on New York, the laws placed a 7 round limit on magazines. Immediately the Governor signed the bill. This led to the instant criminalization of all law enforcement and FBI agents in the State. As no regularly used handguns use 7 round magazines, it was in effect a total handgun ban. No exemption was included for law enforcement.

To be fair to the Governor, the new laws also included mental health checks and other less controversial measures. The law has led to a number of Firearm manufacturers retaliating by refusing to do business with any state run agency. This severely restricts the State Police NYPD and other law enforcement agencies from purchasing Firearms or ammunition from them. The NRA also filed a lawsuit against the State for passing laws that contravened the 2nd Amendment of the United States Constitution.

Pat Quinn

As the Governor of Illinois, the only State in the union that bans concealed carry laws therefore is preventing its residents from defending themselves. And as the State whose capitol city boasts the highest murder rate in the United States you may expect Governor Quinn to be working to make his State safer. However nothing could be further from the truth. Quinn consistently vetoed every bill allowing Concealed carry that reached his desk. Even after the State Supreme Court ordered him to stop infringing the second amendment he continued to resist. In my opinion this Governor is the worst of all of the anti- gun politicians in the USA at this time of writing.

His continued obstruction of any law backing personal defense, together with a reluctance to take on the criminal elements, has led to Chicago having the dubious distinction of being bottom of the league when it comes to prosecutions for gun crime. According to case-by-case U.S. Justice Department information obtained under the Freedom of Information Act, there were 52 federal gun prosecutions in Illinois North (Chicago) in 2012, or 5.52 per million in population.
By this measure, compared with the 90 federal judicial districts in the U.S., the prosecution rate in Chicago was the lowest in the country.
Considering that there were 522 people murdered in Chicago in 2012, one would think that the documented lack of enforcement of existing gun laws would be of at least some concern to Governor Quinn, but apparently not so. A large part of the blame for Chicago's murder rate and misery therefore falls squarely on his shoulders.

John Hickenlooper

The Governor of Colorado who took office on January 11, 2011. Hickenlooper was chiefly responsible for passing draconian anti -gun legislation that all but wiped out the Second Amendment in that State. This included bans on so-called assault weapons and magazines that carried over 15 rounds and universal background checks on all purchases.

The so-called tough gun laws led to a legal
challenge and a widespread protest from
manufactures who announced plans to re-locate
from the State to Thousands of Hunters also
cancelling planed for trips to the State. The Loss of
revenue to the State and the effect of increased
unemployment with manufacturers such as Magpul
re-locating, has yet to be determined, as has the
likely political fallout on the Governor and his
fellow liberals at the next election.

Gov. Dannel P. Malloy

As the Governor of Connecticut, the State that is
home to Newtown scene of the Sandy Hook
shootings, it is understandable that Governor
Malloy would want to support legislation that
would tackle the underlying causes of the school
killings. Unfortunately The Governor went with so
many of his liberal colleagues and pushed through
a raft of gun ban legislation that totally ignored the
real issues and supported the moves to outlaw guns
in his State. Of course this prohibition only applies
to the law-abiding gun owners, not the criminal
elements. The legislation adds more than 100
firearms to the state's assault weapons ban and
creates what officials have called, the nation's first
dangerous weapon offender registry as well as
eligibility rules for buying ammunition, including
background checks for all firearms sales.

Banning gun ownership clearly infringes the second amendment and the creation of a gun registry also breaches federal law. None of this of course matters to the Governor who felt he can push these laws through, on the wave of revulsion felt by those in his State. Unfortunately, having sympathy for the victims of Sandy Hook should never be a reason to disregard the Constitution of the United States.

What guns do they want to ban?

We have heard a lot about the so-called Assault weapons and the reader may well question what they are. The answer depends on your particular views. Legally, the term Assault weapon is not clearly defined, an attempt under the old Assault weapons ban defined an assault weapon as follows;

The term, assault weapon, when used in the context of the assault weapon law of 1994, refers primarily (but not exclusively) to semi-automatic firearms that possessed the cosmetic features of one that is fully automatic. Of course fully automatic weapons were controlled by other laws and still are.

In the original U.S. law, the legal term *assault weapon* included certain specific semi-automatic firearm models by name.

This included Colt AR 15 TEC-9 and the non-select fire AK47 produced by three manufacturers, as well as Uzis and other semi-automatic firearms because they possess a minimum set of cosmetic features from the following list of features: Semi Automatic rifles able to accept detachable magazines and two or more of the following:
Folding or Telescopic Stock
A pistol grip
A bayonet mount
A flash suppressor
A grenade launcher when mounted as a muzzle device \
Semi Auto pistols with detachable magazines, that also includes a magazine that attaches outside the pistol grip
A threaded barrel to attach extenders, flash suppressors, or handgrip
A semi automatic version of a fully automatic firearm
A weapon not exceeding a weight of 50 oz.
A barrel shroud that can double as a handhold

A glance at the above specifications can in part reveal the thrust of the law is that if it looks scary then we will ban it. The ban also defined banned shotguns, as a semi automatic shotgun with a folding stock or pistol grip.

The 1994 ban expired in 2004 after experts conceded it had absolutely no effect on gun crime.

Historically the term assault weapon was first used in the closing stages of WW2 with the introduction of the STG-44 Sturm Gewehr (Storm Rifle) semi auto rifle, looking aesthetically similar to the later AK47. Adolf Hitler dubbed the new rifle, Assault Rifle.

It has been argued that any weapon used by the military can be dubbed an Assault weapon. That would include weapons that range from the Brown Bess muskets used in the War of Independence to the tomahawk used by North American Indians, and US Special Forces in Vietnam.

Many US citizens, me included, own an AK47 and AR 15s in their original specification, as issued in the Vietnam conflict; these weapons have been converted to semi auto only. But apart from that, they look and operate as the originals. To all intents and purposes they are historic weapons. The AK 47 is the worlds most famous and iconic weapon of all time, and also the most mass-produced. That fact alone makes it a must for any serious collector. First manufactured in 1947 the rifle is clearly part of the world's firearm history. In addition to the above-mentioned firearms, the 94/2004 Assault weapons ban also outlawed magazines, containing 10 or more rounds.
The often-used arguments against these guns are that they have no use for hunting and therefore are not covered by the Second Amendment.

This would be true if the Second Amendment was written with hunting in mind. It was not. The Second Amendment makes no mention of hunting, it was written to ensure that the citizens of this country are able to defend themselves. This fact was made abundantly clear in numerous papers penned by the founding fathers and copied in the 13 colonies State constitutions. I am often asked why I need a, quote," Assault" weapon to defend myself. My answer is the same reason that Law enforcement and the secret service need them. The criminals can and do carry them, and we need to be adequately armed to defend ourselves against them. As the gun laws only apply to the law abiding, every new gun law or restriction imposed weakens our ability to defend ourselves. A fact well understood by Madison which is why the law expressly forbids lawmakers from infringing upon those rights.

The Second Amendment to the Constitution of the United States could hardly be clearer. *"The Right of the people to keep and bear Arms shall not be infringed."* It does not say should not or might not be, or even is desired to be. It Says SHALL NOT. I fail to understand why politicians cannot comprehend such a clear instruction.
There is no doubt that the progressive movement in the country will continue to press the issue of gun control.

There is also little doubt that there will be other shootings in the government created target rich environment's that we call gun free zones, or as some call them human arcades. I fear that only a political revolution to sweep these lawmakers from power will change things for the better. The evidence clearly shows that allowing people to carry and use firearms to defend themselves has a dramatic result in decreasing the crime and death rates in the USA.

What can we expect if the gun control supporters get their wish and the Second Amendment is finally abandoned? We will find out in the next 2 chapters.

Chapter 14

Life in the Post
Second Amendment World

"And what country can preserve its liberties, if its rulers are not warned from time to time that this people preserve the spirit of resistance? Let them take arms....The tree of liberty must be refreshed from time to time, with the blood of patriots and tyrants"

(Thomas Jefferson in a letter to William S. Smith in 1787.)

It was midday when the federal agents arrived, at the camp. They moved into the settlement asking the residents to hand over all weapons that were being confiscated. *For their own safety and protection.* Some were unhappy and protested that they needed guns to protect themselves but the authorities were in no mood to listen. The majority handed over their guns as a unit of heavily armed US Army troops stood by in case of trouble. An incident sparked a mass shooting, suddenly troops were firing wildly, and rifle, pistol, and indiscriminate cannon fire tore into the camp residents.

When the smoke cleared 297 lay dead, 200 of them women and children, 27 US troops were also dead, most killed by their own sides' wild shooting with the Hotchkiss cannons.

Where did this mass murder occur, Afghanistan, Iraq, or North Korea maybe?

No this occurred in the United States in South Dakota. At a place that's name still reverberates down through the years. A place that was a peaceful Native American winter camp close to a Reservation called Pine Ridge. The place was Wounded Knee, and the date December 29th 1890. Philip Wells was a mixed blood Lakota Sioux who was employed as an interpreter for the troop's commander Colonel Forsyth, commanding the famed US 7th Cavalry. The unit that had been decimated by the Sioux 14 years earlier in another battle in South Dakota called Little Big Horn. The commander at that battle, Col. George Armstrong Custer had been killed and it was his successor whose troops carried out the killings. After the massacre he gave this vivid account.

The captured Indians had been ordered to give up their arms, but Chief Big Foot had replied that his people had no arms. Forsyth said to me, 'Tell Big Foot he says the Indians have no arms, yet yesterday they were well armed when they surrendered. He is deceiving me. Tell him he need have no fear in giving up his arms, as I wish to treat him kindly.'

Big Foot replied, 'They have no guns, except such as you have found.' Forsyth declared, 'You are lying to me in return for my kindness. 'Forsyth and I went to the circle of warriors where he told me to tell the medicine man to sit down and keep quiet, but he paid no attention to the order. Forsyth repeated the order. Big Foot's brother-in-law answered, 'He will sit down when he gets around the circle.' When the medicine man came to the end of the circle, he squatted down. A cavalry sergeant exclaimed, 'There goes an Indian with a gun under his blanket!' Forsyth ordered him to take the gun from the Indian, which he did. Whitside then said to me, 'Tell the Indians it is necessary that they be searched one at a time.' The young warriors paid no attention to what I told them. I heard someone on my left exclaim, 'Look out! Look out!' I saw five or six young warriors cast off their blankets and pull guns out from under them and brandish them in the air. One of the warriors shot into the soldiers, who were ordered to fire into the Indians. I looked in the direction of the medicine man. He or some other medicine man approached to within three or four feet of me with a long cheese knife, ground to a sharp point and raised to stab me. He stabbed me during the melee and nearly cut off my nose. I held him off until I could swing my rifle to hit him, which I did. I shot and killed him in self-defense.

Troop 'K' was drawn up between the tents of the women and children and the main body of the Indians, who had been summoned to deliver their arms. The Indians began firing into 'Troop K' to gain the canyon of Wounded Knee creek. In doing so they exposed their women and children to their own fire. Captain Wallace was killed at this time while standing in front of his troops. A bullet, striking him in the forehead, plowed away the top of his head. I started to pull off my nose, which was hung by the skin, but Lieutenant Guy Preston shouted, 'My God Man! Don't do that! That can be saved.' He then led me away from the scene of the trouble."

It will never be known why Col. Forsyth launched the attack. Was it out of necessity or maybe revenge? Philip Wells account clearly shows that the younger members of the tribe did not trust the Army and had no intention of being disarmed; they tried to hide some of the guns. Would modern gun owners act the same way?

Although this incident occurred 120 years ago, it does give an insight into what could happen if gun confiscation becomes a reality, if Police units who have suffered casualties, are commanded to move in and seize guns from the public.
A wise politician once said, *"Those that do not learn from the mistakes of history are destined to repeat them."*

One can argue that today's modern army is not what it was in 1890. That is true, but Incidents such as Mi Lai in Vietnam and Abu Grade in Iraq show us that we are not perfect. Often emotions get in the way of rational thought. The right of the people to keep and bear arms should never be interpreted by politicians no matter what party they belong to. It is a fundamental right granted to each and every American under the Constitution of the United States.

We need to fight constantly to keep that right in the current climate, but that fighting should be done via the Ballot Box and the professional shooters in the Country. I recall a few years ago in England, I was asked by a political friend to attend a Political meeting called by representatives of the European Union. The speakers were sent to persuade us that we would be much better off if we allowed Germany, France, and Europe to decide British Policy. I attended to 'explain' that we did neither want nor need their control.

I listened to the speakers in silence, though it was obvious the crowd was not on board with their ideas. When it came my time to speak I stood up and addressed the smartly dressed Eurocrat directly.

I told him that his ideas of European control were unwelcome here and that I would fight him and his kind until hell freezes over, because I would rather fight him now in the ballot box than in 10 years with a rifle in my hands. For that outburst I got a standing ovation, and a personal invitation from the leader of the UKIP to join his party. I also had the satisfaction of seeing the speakers cancel the question and answer session and flee the hall to the jeers of the audience.

In the 1970s I was shooting regularly in the United Kingdom at competitions and often visited neighboring gun clubs. At one such club I became friends with a club official, I will not name him for reasons that will become clear later. But will refer to him as Mike. Suffice it to say, we shot together regularly and I learned a lot about handgun shooting from him. Mike was an excellent shot and frequently outshot me. Often we would sit in the club bar and debate the gun controls. As I was a cop Mike often questioned me about legal matters, or maybe it is more correct to say argued with me. Nevertheless mike and I remained friends. I was posted away from Aldershot in the early 1980s and saw him less frequently. Following my departure from the Police I lost contact with him altogether. In May 2009 I received a phone call from my ex wife, at my home in Kentucky to tell me that Mike was dead. He had apparently been shot by police at a sheltered flat he shared with his sick wife.

The news stunned me and I immediately looked into the circumstances. It appears that on May 9th 2009 Mike who was 64, was at home with his wife, and was upset that her condition had deteriorated to the extent that she was to be confined in a nursing home. Mike who was still an avid gun guy, but under the new gun ban in UK he was restricted to owning a colt 45 black powder gun. According to evidence given at the inquest, mike had threatened the Nursing assistant who came to tell him the news, and stated that no one was going to take his wife away.

After the police arrived threats were shouted and a 3-hour standoff ensued. Finally the police made an entry and found Mike lying on his bed, they pulled his covers off, and mike opened fire. The officers returned fire, striking Mike once in the chest.

This was a sad end for a man who had lived for his shooting. Without knowing the full circumstances it would be wrong of me to criticize the Police actions. There was a great deal of anger from his family and neighbors at the killing.

I know that at least one commentator offered the theory that this could have been a suicide by cop scenario. This is a virtually unknown occurrence in the UK where the general Police force is unarmed. But it does happen in the USA. I do recall Mike telling me on more than one occasion that he would fight anyone trying to take his guns away; so maybe.

Australia also banned its citizens from owning guns, and this was also done in the wake of a mass shooting and it too had little effect on gun violence.
Most people in the USA and Europe have never heard the name Rodney Ansell; he never became famous or got elected to high office. Rodney was an Australian whose exploits inspired filmmaker Paul Faiman to direct Crocodile Dundee, a film based loosely on his exploits.

Ansell first came to notice in 1977 when he wandered out of the wilderness into the town of Top End, having survived for several days with little or no resources. In 1979, filmmaker Richard Oxenburgh asked Ansell to relive his adventures in the documentary film *To Fight the Wild*, which the following year was published as a book. Although both accepted Ansell's version of events uncritically, his story was frequently treated with skepticism by locals in Top End. Some were convinced that the whole story was a publicity stunt. Others wondered why and experienced outback man like Ansell did not simply follow the river downstream to the nearest town.

When Ansell was asked in interviews what he was doing in the remote Australian wilderness by himself, he claimed he was on a fishing trip. Privately, however, he confided to friends that he was actually poaching crocodiles.

The story would not have gained any wider publicity had it not been for The BBC.

In 1981, Ansell was invited to come to Sydney to be interviewed by famed English journalist Michael Parkinson for an episode of the BBC Television program 'Parkinson'. In typical Crocodile Dundee fashion Ansell attended the interview barefoot. The station put him up at The Sebel Townhouse Hotel, a 5 star hotel in downtown Sydney. While there, he came to the staffs' attention by sleeping on the floor in a sleeping bag rather than using the bed and was reportedly mystified by his room's bidet. Ansell's interview and curious city antics sparked Paul Hogan's interest, inspiring him and co-writers Ken Shadie, and John Cornell to create the character of Mick crocodile Dundee.

According to Ansell's friends, he was "at one" with Arnhem Lands Aborigines, and like the film character, he spoke Urapunga fluently, having become a "fully initiated white man." Fame quickly followed. Ansell was named Territorian of the Year in 1987 for helping to put Top End on the world map. However, Ansell's newfound fame alienated him from his peers, and he late lamented of his rejection back home.

This account was first published in November 2000 edition of The Firing Line. It is reprinted in part here,

'Last August, Rodney William Ansell, the rugged Aussie whose real life exploits inspired the Crocodile Dundee movies, died in a shootout with Australian police who had come (to confiscate his unregistered firearms. Oh, you didn't read about it in our 'free' press? That's cause it never appeared.

A police sergeant was also killed in the incident; the number of "peace officers" injured while invading old 'Croc' in his natural domain is unknown, but likely he took down several. I don't mean to imply glee over the death and possible additional injuries; after all, they were "just doing their job" like the obedient Nazi's tried at Nuremburg.

Ansell had been named 1988 Australian Man of the Year for inspiring the movie and putting Australia on the Tourism Map." of particular interest to us here in the tourism dependent desert, Ansell was probably responsible for hundreds of millions of increased tourism dollars flowing into his beloved country. This is how his country repaid him. Because you see, in today's world, no good deed goes unpunished and no bad deed un-rewarded. After all, Janet Reno was the laughingstock of DA's nation-wide for her inept to outright unlawful per-formance in Florida.

She is now "our-Attorney General (in addition to Fidel Castro's

What motivated this shooting? In 1996, Australia adopted draconian gun control laws banning 60% of all firearms and requiring registration of all firearms and licensing of gun owners. As a result, Rod Ansell believed that police were coming to confiscate his unregistered firearms. In Australia today, police do not need a search warrant to enter your house and search for guns. Police can search door-to-door looking for un-surrendered weapons in their gun buyback program. They have been using previous gun regis-tration and license lists to check for non-compliance and confiscate now illegal firearms. The rush to draft stringent gun controls in Australia, in a curious foreshadowing of our own post-Columbine experience began after, in 1996, a crazed gunman shot 35 people. Australians were shocked, and the government reacted quickly. Draconian gun legislation was passed in the heat of the moment.

Notes former California State Senator H.L. Richardson "They outlawed every semi-auto, even those pretty duck guns, pump shotguns and semi-auto hunting rifles.

"They didn't miss a one. In today's Australia, it is illegal for any citizen except officers to own even .22's and sporting shotguns designed for duck hunting."

The result? As in Great Britain, crime has escalated beyond belief! In the year following implementation of the law, Australia experienced a 44% increase in armed robberies, 8.6% Increase in assaults and a ~ increase in homicides. In the state of Victoria there was a 300% increase in firearm homicides!!!l In South Australia, robberies increased 58%. Two years after the ban, according to the Australian Bureau of Statistics, Armed robberies are up 73% and assaults are up 17%. By comparison, in the 25 years before the ban, Australia had a steady decrease both in firearm homicides and robberies. It is now a haven heaven for every criminal creep who knows there's little chance law-abiding citi-zens can defend themselves. The police can't prevent crime or protect & serve you until it's too late, - dead men and women can't dial 911. Ominously, the history of Australia in many ways parallels that of the U.S. In the 1860's it had pioneering settlers like our own Western migration. In World War I and II, it fought with the Allies. Australia remained subject to Great Britain until 1986, when the last ties with the U.K. were dissolved. With just 19 million people, Australia has an impressive fauna including plenty of varmints like marsupials and dingoes which wreak havoc on ranchers' livestock. Yet hunting and Varmint eradication is prohibited for all but a handful of rich and connected Australians.

Good-bye and God-Bless you Rod "Crocodile" Ansell. I only wish I could have met you before your legal murder.
Special thanks to Miguel Faria Jr., M.D., Editor-in-Chief of the Journal of American Physicians and Surgeons, for providing the information and documentation that made this story possible. +
NOTE: Unfortunately, the author's name was not included. I respectfully submit the article in full respect of his/her work and knowing very much that they just want to 'get the word out'.

Whilst it is true that this account is biased and that there is certainly evidence that the circumstances surrounding Ansell's death, are not as clear-cut as 'The Firing line' article would have us believe. Nevertheless Ansell was a proud man who resented the Government's intrusion into what he conceived to be his business. He passionately believed that no politician had a right to take his guns.

Regardless of your views on his demise, those thinking that they can merely stand back and shoot at anyone attempting to take their guns, should take note.

Although the 'Firing Line' account is accurate in its broad outline, what was left out is that Ansell had become very bitter since the film, returned to the outback and became mentally unstable.

We have seen such bitterness in other shootings, most recently in February 2013 in the Los Angeles case of ex LAPD officer Christopher Dorner who went on a shooting spree before being surrounded in a cabin at Big Bear.

Obviously in neither Ansell's case nor that of 'Mike' would I condemn the police actions. I wasn't there and police will always be justified in returning fire when shot at.

Often when I meet Second Amendment advocates I hear them say things like, 'Let them try and take my guns', or 'they'll have to pry it from my cold dead hands.'

There is no doubt that if any US government tries total confiscation then a number will put up a Crocodile Dundee last stand, which will end the same way. However, many will not. I do not see the residents of California or New York barricading themselves in their home and trading gunfire with the local PD. That is despite clear infringements of the 2nd Amendment by lawmakers in those jurisdictions.

The worst result of an attempt at disarmament would be the opposition of many County Sheriffs who have threatened to arrest and jail any federal agents or marshals attempting to enforce what they see are clear violations of the US Constitution.

Criminals would of course ignore the law as they always have. They will no doubt look on with amusement at the clownish efforts to stop gun violence by disarming all but the criminals.

Faced with a growing lawlessness and infighting between various State Law Enforcement agencies, civil unrest will become widespread. The popular TV reality show Doomsday Preppers illustrates all too clearly that many Americans are already making preparations for such an event.

I am often asked why the British stood meekly by and allowed the government to take their guns. To understand the answer it is necessary to understand that personal defense has not been considered a valid reason to own a gun in the UK for almost 100 years. Gun owners were given one month to hand in guns and then they faced a mandatory 5 year prison term. Hunting for all but the British Elite had already been banned and there is little opposition to Government control.

Here in the USA the culture is different. Hunting is popular and you have laws based on a Constitution. But supposing the constitution was trashed, that gun rights did not exist, what sort of world would we be living in.

Chapter 15

Mumbai

"Among the many misdeeds of British rule in India, history will look upon the Act depriving a whole nation of arms as the blackest."

Mahatma Mohandas Gandhi

Let's take a look at what happens when a country finally succeeds in utterly stamping out its gun culture. The city of Mumbai, formerly Bombay, is the capital city of the Indian state of Maharashtra. It is the most populous city in India, and the fourth most populous city in the world. While under British Rule the ownership of private firearms was banned. A change in 1959 was made when the new Indian government drafted a law to replace the British one. It granted every citizen the right to bear arms, regardless of race or social standing. It couldn't last of course though. A succession of progressive governments, together with a culture of corruption cut the law to pieces.

By 2008 Mumbai was all but devoid of gun owners. Police were poorly trained; their marksmanship was abysmal due in part to the local anti gun authorities.

The Indian police had no clue as to what to do in the event of an active shooter because they'd never been taught what to do. Their leadership hated and feared the gun so much that they stamped out the ability for any of their men to actually master the tool. When you kill your gun culture, you kill off your instructors, and those who can pass down the information necessary to do the job. Mumbai was now the worlds biggest gun free killing zone. The scene was very reminiscent of the original Judge Dredd movie when a cryogenic Sylvester Stallone was defrosted to deal with a gun-toting terrorist because the Police had never experienced gun crime, and was in an absolute panic.

But anti-gun campaigners said arming citizens is not the way forward. The Control Arms Foundation of India (CAFI), which was set in up 2004 in response to rising gun crime in the northeast. Estimates there are already some 46 million firearms in India, making it the country with the second largest number of guns in civilian hands after the US.

The pro gun lobby point out the majority of these was caused by the 40 million illegal arms in circulation, not the 5 million legal ones. This is similar to the argument used in the US. The scene was set for a massive wake up call. It came on November 26, when 10 men in inflatable speedboats came ashore at two locations in Colaba.

They reportedly told local Marathi speaking fishermen who asked them who they were to "mind their own business" before they split up and headed two different ways. The fishermen were suspicious of the heavily armed men and reported the incident to the Police but there was little response.

The Chhatrapati Shivaji Terminus was the first target attacked. Two gunmen entered the building, moved into the crowded passenger hall, and opened fire using AK 47 rifles. The attackers killed 58 people and injured 104 others. They met no resistance. Police and emergency services arrived after the attack and as the terrorists were leaving the scene the two gunmen opened fire on the police and pedestrians, killing eight police officers. The attackers passed a police station. Many of the outgunned police officers were afraid to confront the attackers, and instead switched off the lights and secured the gates. Emboldened, the attackers then headed towards Cama Hospital intending to kill as many patients, but the hospital staff locked all of the patient wards.

Meanwhile a team of the Mumbai Anti-Terrorist Squad led by police Chief Hemant Karkare reached Chhatrapati Shivaji Terminus and realizes then left in pursuit of the gunmen. The two terrorists opened fire on the police vehicle.

The police returned fire; four police officers including Karkare were killed. The only survivor, Constable Arun Jadhav, was wounded, but managed to get off a radio call for help. In an effort to escape, the two gunmen seized the police vehicle but later abandoned it and seized a passenger car instead. Then their luck ran out. They ran into a police roadblock which had been set up after Jadhav radioed for help. Another deadly gun battle erupted. One terrorist was killed and the other, Kasab, was wounded after a physical struggle was arrested. Kasab was the only survivor of the two.

An Indian police officer was also killed in the battle.

The second target attacked by the terrorists was the Leopold Café, a popular restaurant with both tourists and locals, located in the Colaba Causeway in the south of the city. Two terrorists walked into the premises and opened fire with automatic weapons. Ten diners were killed before the attackers moved on.

The main targets for the terrorists were two hotels. The terrorists converged on the Taj Mahal Palace and Tower and the Oberoi Trident armed with bombs, automatic weapons, and grenades.

Six explosions tore apart the Taj hotel - one in the lobby, two in the elevators and three more in the restaurant causing mass casualties. At the same time, another explosion was reported at the Oberoi Trident.

At the Taj Mahal, The terrorists were holding hostages and both hotels were eventually surrounded by Rapid Action Force personnel and Marine Commandos (MARCOS) together with National Security Guards (NSG) commandos. Security forces stormed both hotels, and all nine attackers were killed. City firefighters rescued 200 hostages from windows using ladders during first night.

Azam Amir Kasav

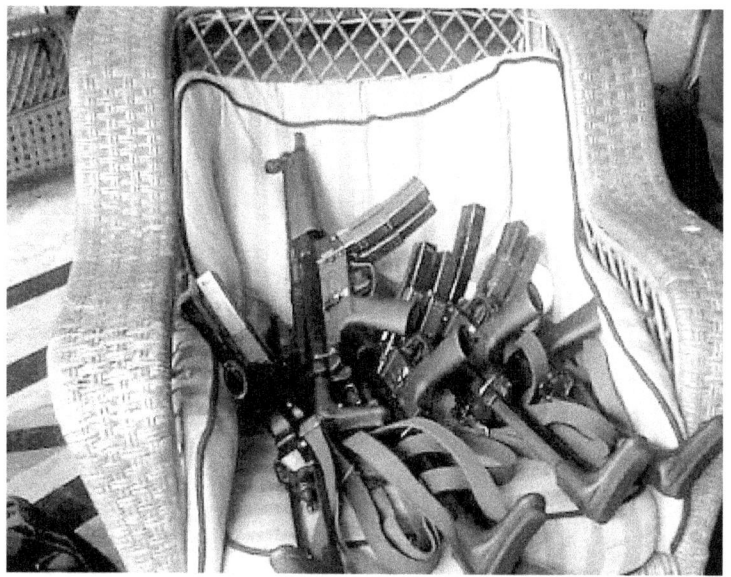
Recovered weapons after the massacre

Nariman House, a Chabad-Lubavitch Jewish center in Colaba known locally as the Mumbai Chabad House, was taken over by two attackers and several of its residents were held hostage. Police evacuated the adjacent buildings and exchanged fire with the attackers, wounding one. The attackers threw a grenade into a nearby lane, causing no casualties. NSG commandos arrived from Delhi, and a naval helicopter took an aerial survey. During the first day, security forces managed to rescue 9 hostages from the first floor. The following day, the house was stormed by NSG commandos fast roping from helicopters onto the roof, covered by snipers positioned in nearby buildings. After a long battle, one NSG commando and both perpetrators were killed.

However there had been a price to pay, a Rabbi, and his wife who was six months pregnant, were murdered with four other hostages inside the house by the attackers. Injuries reported on some of the bodies indicate they may have been tortured.

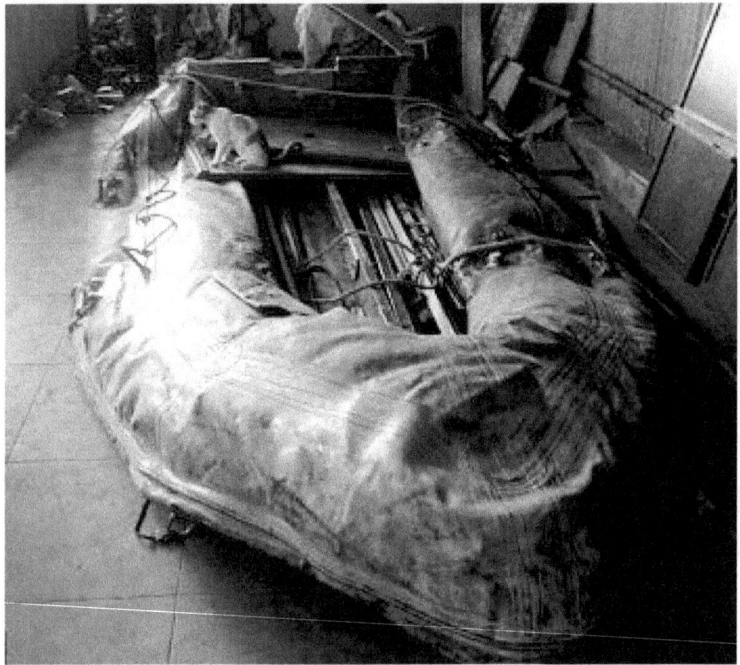

The inflatable boat used by the terrorists at Mumbai

A total of 166 people died in these attacks. The sole terrorist survivor was later tried, convicted, and hanged.

All of the attackers were Pakistani Nationals and there were strong indications that the Pakistani Government was less than enthusiastic about investigating the terrorist group or its infrastructure. A trend we saw repeated after the Killing of Osama Bin Laden, in a Pakistani compound where he had been living for some considerable time.

A look at the gun laws in India reveals some startling similarities with certain US States Cities.

Rakshit Sharma is the secretary-general of the National Association for Gun Rights, India (NAGRI), which was formed by "public spirited" people who wanted to counter the "policy of creeping disarmament of law abiding citizens." He offers the following synopsis of the gun legislation in his country.

"The law in India basically states that any Indian of sound mind, good character, with no criminal record and a safe place to keep the weapon can get a license. But when you try to apply for one, it is almost impossible to get it. This happens in 99 per cent of the cases. Why is the government trying to take the gun out of the hands of the legal gun owner? Criminals don't apply for gun licenses; they go to the grey market. There is also a lot of anti-gun propaganda. "

When weapons are recovered following a case these weapons become the property of the court (State). But later, they are auctioned off to politicians and senior officials.
In India, 37 percent of lawmakers have criminal backgrounds. The culture of corruption in India makes the whole issue of gun control murky at best.

It took Sharma three years to get a license. He now owns a .32 caliber revolver. He doesn't believe most Indians would back stricter gun control. The process of getting a license is so tedious that many are deterred by the lengthy process. Even if you get the license, the cheapest gun costs ₹ 75,000 ($1,400) which would not even sell for $75 in the international market. Any decent imported gun costs not less than ₹600,000, ($11,000). This same weapon would cost $200 in the international market. Most gun owners can get only 25 cartridges a year. And at one time, you could only buy ten. This applies to competitive shooters too! Ammo is costly; a single imported round costs ₹500, ($9.00). So if you fire off 10 rounds, it will cost you ₹5,000, ($92.00).

Chapter 16

Solutions and a Path to Sanity

So far we have explored the aspect of the mass killings across the world. I have been pretty contemptuous of the politicians who are pushing through their gun control agenda and have no problem putting the lives of our children and citizens at risk in order to further their agenda. You may well ask that if banning guns is not the answer, then what is.

To find the answer we need to accept that we are unlikely to ever prevent a madman going over the edge. If we could do so then we could revolutionize the mental health treatment, not only here but across the world. However there are people and organizations that are working to recognize the danger signs and threat indicators and this seems to be an advance forward. One of the more encouraging steps taken since the tragic events at Sandy Hook was the setting up of the School Shield Program. This project is funded but not operated by the National Rifle Association. They took a long hard look at not just Sandy Hook, but other schools around the country.
In early April 2013 Former congressman Isa Hutchinson, the man selected by the NRA to head up a school safety program, released his report.

The report was immediately condemned by most of the Liberal media groups and anti gun advocates. Most of course, judging by their responses, had never read it. The report was not a statement by the NRA, though it is true that they paid $1 million to fund the research.

In 225 pages the report recommended eight target goals to improve school safety, including a 40-60 hour training program for school resource officers and armed school personnel, revisions to state laws allowing personnel to carry guns, improving cooperation between law enforcement officials and schools, and giving schools access to online tools on safety policies. The study also proposed making school safety a priority of state educational requirements, increasing federal funding for developing school safety initiatives, turning the "Shield Program" into a permanent group, and creating a pilot program to assess threats and mental health.

Hutchinson guaranteed the report maintained "full independence" from the NRA, saying, "There's no guarantee the NRA will accept these recommendations." The NRA itself issued the following response:
"We need time to digest the full report.

We commend Isa Hutchinson for his rapid response in the aftermath of the Newtown tragedy, and we are certain the contributions he and his team have made will go a long way to making America's schools safer."

So what is actually in the report? The first pages detail the recognition of threat assessments and Threat indicators, referring to data already carried out by the FBI and DHS. They identify lax procedures such as CCTV cameras often being poorly placed and having items place in the way which restricts a good field of view. The study also found instances of poor car park surveillance and perimeter fencing in disrepair.

Attention was paid to practices such as school bussing procedures and visitor reception. The report also addresses the implementation of incident response teams and the implementation of lockdown procedures. Isa Hutchinson and his team have been very thorough in their analysis of the response to the problem. It is not until page 93 of the report that mention is made of armed personnel. It states firmly that the decision to arm guards or staff is one for the school alone. However it does suggest the following qualifications on any applicants resume.
Former employment data;

•

DMV records;

- Residential address history verification;
- Credit check;
- Criminal records check;
- Education verification;
- Civil history;
- National wants and warrants;
- Social security verification;
- Drug testing;
- Finger print screening

The report also recommends that schools conduct a periodic background check on all security personnel upon hiring and at least once every three years. If a more in-depth pre-employment background screening is desired, it is recommended that the school contact a local private investigator.

There are four primary possibilities in terms of arming personnel in schools.
They are as follows,

<u>School Resource Officers</u>

<u>Private Contracted Security</u>

<u>Armed Citizen Volunteers</u>

<u>Arming school staff and teachers,</u>

Each of these possibilities has both pros and cons. The School Shield program addresses these concerns in a well-balanced way. While reading through the report I was struck by the meticulous way the various issues have been addressed. This is the same attention to detail carried out by law enforcement officers when investigating a case, and as a former law enforcement officer I can appreciate the work that has gone into the study.

The following persons comprised the consulting team for the School Shield Program.

Mr. Ralph Basham
Former Director of US Secret Service (USSS), Former Commissioner of US Customs and Border Protection (CBP), Former Chief of Staff of US Transportation Security Administration (TSA), Former Director of Federal Law Enforcement Training Center (FLETC)
•
Mr. Thad Bingel

Former Chief of Staff of US Customs and Border Protection (CBP)

•

Mr. Bruce Bowen
Former Deputy Director of US Secret Service, Former Assistant Director of Federal Law Enforcement Training Center (FLETC)

•

Mr. Mike Restovich
Former Chief Homeland Security Attaché of US Embassy in London, Former Assistant Administrator of US Transportation Security Administration (TSA)

•

Colonel (ret.) John Quattrone
US Air Force (USAF) Security Forces Officer, Former three time Commander,
Former Joint Staff Operations Antiterrorism/Homeland Defense Directorate, The Pentagon

•

Mr. Tony Lambraia
CEO of Phoenix RBT Solutions

•

Mr. Robert Lambraia
Director of Training of Phoenix RBT Solutions

•

Mr. Joe Overstreet
Former US Secret Service Special Agent, Law Enforcement Training Manger of Phoenix RBT Solutions

-

Mr. Randy Knapp
Instructor RBT Solutions

-

Mr. Joseph Turitto
Retired Police Sergeant

-

Mr. Wence Arevalo
Police SWAT/Entry Team Leader Sergeant

The report also gives numerous examples of bad practices and lax security practices in the schools the researchers visited. These are illustrated by photographs and diagrams. In all, the team have done a good job and have shown a deep understanding of the problems.

This is in such sharp contrast to ill thought out policies of some states to rush to pass gun ban or gun restriction legislation with little or no thought to the consequences. Some even accepted that such legislation would be unlikely to prevent any future shootings, but they went ahead anyway.

School Shield has been well received by the parents and school authorities in general but not by the anti gun politicians who daily show their true agenda. We must not allow them to thwart efforts to protect our children.

I am also encouraged that efforts to bring an end to gun free zones are being continually brought up by politicians, mostly Republicans. This is a shame, as such a serious issue as the safety of our children should come down to party line politics. At the time of writing there is a serious push by the Democratic Party to force through severe restrictions on gun ownership. This support is coming from the White House and the liberal media. The Second Amendment is being overruled by many Governor's and city mayors. This will of course lead to lawsuits from the NRA and other groups. All of which will cost time and money. More importantly it will drive a deeper wedge between both Republican and Democrats. This in turn will make the business of solving our Nations troubles even more complex. The one area that may help is in the contentious issue of background checks for gun purchases. This is opposed by the NRA on the grounds that criminals will not be subject to the checks. Also, the records of the mentally ill are not part of the database that is used for background checks. Most medical professionals support the exemption on the grounds of patient confidentiality. With such data excluded there seems little value in the checks. They would not identify potential risk threats and known criminals would not try to pass a check anyway. If we are serious about wanting to protect our children then we must make some bold decisions.

This will mean spending money and replacing politically motivated lawmakers with those committed to policies that have been shown to work. We also need to look at the violent culture depicted on TV and Films. I am not advocating censorship. I personally enjoy a good action film where the hero, equipped with a stunning array of weaponry can outshoot his villainous opponents and emerge victorious. However we must recognize that the exposure of children to such scenes will put their developing minds under a great deal of pressure. My friend Lt. Col. Dave Grossman explores this theme in his book, *"Are we teaching our kids to kill."* Of course the advent of the violent video game has heightened the problem. In my book "Compulsion to Kill" I explored the link with the serial gun killers and Video games' noting that addiction to such games is one of the common traits of these individuals.

Keeping these games out of the hands of children is not an easy task. But that does not mean we should not try. I would favor controls similar to those enacted to restrict alcohol to minors.

Requirements before purchase can be made and stiff penalties to anyone supplying such games to minors. Take away or restrict the fun sporting element of killing people and you will see more sensible decisions being made.

The Gun Free Killing Zones of America

Conclusion

In this book I have tried to lay out the inherent dangers to not just our schools but to the whole concept of Gun Free Zones. I have never understood why, despite overwhelming evidence and a rising body count, politicians continue to promote and even expand the areas where the lone crazed gunman can carry out their gruesome task. Having discounted the idea that they are just too dumb or subscribing to the fanciful conspiracy theory that this is part of a dastardly take over plan by the communists, Muslims of any other group; I have come to the conclusion that this is more political than practical.

There are politicians who are convinced that the job of Government is to control the Population. In most countries in the developed world, that view is incompatible with allowing the population to possess firearms. The USA is the exception; it is a union of States bound a Constitution that includes a bill of Rights with the Right to keep and bear Arms at its core.

Apart from the United States Constitution. Most States have also adopted a right to keep and bear arms as part of their own constitutions.

The right to keep and bear arms was included in the national and State constitutions for one reason only, the people demanded it and the States would not have agreed to a Union without it.
James Madison who wrote the Bill of Rights, made plain in several papers and letters written at the time, that the reason for its inclusion was nothing to do with hunting or target shooting, or recreational sports. It was a protection against the tyranny of Government. This inconvenient fact is usually overlooked or ignored by present day politicians but was well understood by the Founding Fathers. Several of whom wrote in support of it. Including, George Washington, and Thomas Jefferson.

The war of independence was started over the British attempting to seize guns from colonists at Lexington and Concord in 1775. Having won the war against the most powerful empire on earth, the fledgling Americans were hardly likely to surrender their Arms to another Government. They had learned the bitter lesson that Freedom is never free, it is paid for by the blood of the people who fight for it.

The wave of gun control hysteria following tragedies such as Virginia Tech, Columbine, and Sandy Hook is understandable from the families of the victims, but to make gun control effective in reducing crime, all guns would need to be banned.

And that ban enforced. When I say all guns, I mean just that. No guns for the Armed Forces, Law Enforcement, and Security. Every house searched and every weapon collected and destroyed.

That would eliminate the threat of mass killing by guns, but not of course the threat of mass killing. I hardly need to point out the flaws of this scenario. Some of you may even say, what about the criminal who hides his guns? Aha! Do I see a light come on here!

Ok! Enough of the fantasy utopia of the gun control gang let us return to the real world. There are over 100 million gun owners in the USA. Law enforcement require to be well armed to do their job properly and law abiding armed citizens shoot four times as many bad guys, as do cops.
The statement by NRA vice President Wayne La Pierre, that the only thing that stops a bad man with a gun, is a good man with a gun, is true. It matters not, whether the good man is a cop, a soldier, or an armed citizen. This causes a problem for the bad guy. If he breaks into a house at night he runs the risk of encountering an armed response from a homeowner who is likely to shoot first, and ask questions later. But as we have seen, the bad guys are not only the dishonest criminals or sexual predators.

There is a new breed of criminal, the thrill killer, the terrorist whose agenda is political ideology. The prime motive for such people is a high body count, the highest they can achieve. They do not expect to survive the incident. To achieve their aim they look for the location that will give them the targets they need. They look for a large crowded area, with little or no security and if possible with the maximum impact on the community they are seeking to punish.

The Gun Free Zone ticks all the boxes. They provide a target rich environment where the government has ensured that no one will be armed to shoot back, '*The Human Arcade*'.

The United States of America is undergoing political and social changes at present. We have seen this in the mass shootings at schools and at Fort Hood. I do not profess to be able to predict what the future is for the Second Amendment and the right we all have to self-defense. There are politicians who do not or will not accept that disarming the people will lead to a blood bath. It is in turbulent times such as this that dictators and despots often rise to take power. The solution to all our differences must lie in the democratic process. I have never been impressed with the argument that we resort to armed resistance if the Government try to ban our guns.

I heard the same arguments in England. If you disagree with a policy then do not vote for the person that advocates it. Ask any gun owner you know if they want to keep their guns, and then ask them who they voted for.

Almost half the country did not vote. The majority voted for a political party that by and large is anti-gun. This is a problem. I leave you with this thought.

If you did not bother to vote in the last election, then you have lost the right to express any opinion as to the outcome. That will upset many readers but there will be the ones who did not vote.

Stephen Challis 2013.

Credits
Lt Col Dave Grossman US Army retired. The Libertarian Party. Suzanna Gratia Hupp (From Lubys to the legislature) Newtown Police Dept. Evan M Todd. John Lott (National Review on Line). The National Rifle Association. Terror at Beslan by John Giduck. . Newtown Police Department. Debarred the Use of Arms - Compulsion to kill Stephen Challis. Amazon, Outskirts Press. Colonel Terry Lee US army Rtd. Charles Allen, former under secretary of Homeland Security. Sergeant Michal Davis US Army. Mayor Harry Moore. Mark Meeker. Assault Weapons Control Act of 1989. The Gun Free Zones Act 1990. Philip Wells (US 7th Cavalry 1890) .2000 edition The Firing Line. Rakshit Sharma is the secretary-general of the National Association for Gun Rights, India. Photo Credits. James Pozark, Vladikavkaz ossezia Delnord. Associated Press. All illustrations public domain unless stated.